STRAIGHT LINES
—for—
PARENTS

Strategies for Raising Exceptional Kids

by
Drs. Steve & Rebecca Wilke

All Scripture quotations are taken from the HOLY BIBLE, NEW INTERNATIONAL VERSION®. NIV®. Copyright©1973, 1978, 1984 by the International Bible Society. Used by permission of Zondervan. All rights reserved.

*Please note: Confidentiality is a priority for us, so we have changed many names of individuals in the stories that follow.

Straight Lines for Parents: 9 Strategies for Raising Exceptional Kids
Copyright 2012 by Drs. Steve and Rebecca Wilke

Published by Sonkist Publishing
SONKIST MINISTRIES
P.O. Box 503377
San Diego, CA 92150
www.sonkist.com

Publisher's Cataloging-in-Publication Data
(Provided by Cassidy Cataloguing Services, Inc.)

Wilke, Steve (Stephen D.)

    Straight lines for parents : 9 strategies for raising exceptional kids / by Steve & Rebecca Wilke. -- 1st ed. -- Nashville, TN : ACW Press, c2012.

        p. ; cm.
        ISBN: 978-0-9852112-0-2
        Includes bibliography.

        1. Child rearing—Religious aspects—Christianity. 2. Parenting—Religious aspects—Christianity. 3. Child rearing. 4. Parenting. I. Wilke, Rebecca Lynn. II. Title.

BV4529 .W55 2012
248.845--dc23   1207

All rights reserved. No part of this book may be reproduced in any form without permission from Sonkist Ministries.

Printed in the United States of America.

*Listen, my son, accept what I say, and the years
of your life will be many. I instruct you in the way
of wisdom and lead you along straight paths.
When you walk, your steps will not be hampered;
when you run, you will not stumble.*

Proverbs 4:10–12

Contents

Preface 7
Acknowledgements 9

1. Straight Lines are Intentional 13
2. It's All About Faith 27
3. Family Matters 47
4. Discipline to Self-Disciplined 65
5. Relationship as Center of Our Universe 85
6. Education Develops Exceptional Kids 101
7. Personal Responsibility and Parenting 119
8. Life Experience and Your Exceptional Child 139
9. Leaving a Lasting Legacy 159
10. Summing Up Straight Line Strategies 179

Resources 193
About the Authors 195

Preface

Parenting is all about "Straight Lines," and these specific guidelines will greatly enhance your effectiveness no matter how many children you have, how old they are, or what your marital status may be. We like to define Straight Lines as those deep-rooted principles that don't waiver. Sometimes we call them values, or morals, or standards. Basically, they are just like the boundary lines on a roadway that keep you on course so you don't drift the wrong direction, harming yourself and others.

Straight Line Strategies are more important than ever for parents living in the world today. Since the mid-twentieth century, people have been trying to parent in the midst of major cultural shifts—everything from Dr. Spock to the sexual revolution to social networking have been pushing and pulling at traditional values and time-tested parenting skills.

In addition, our society has been inundated with new ideas and spurious "ideals" about how kids should be raised. Some child development experts have even suggested a "hands off" approach—in other words, letting kids grow, develop, and express themselves without much in the way of strategic instruction or guidance. Sadly, we've seen some of the catastrophic results of this parental abandonment in modern culture.

We firmly believe that successful parenting is an *intentional process*, and clear-cut guidelines will get you started on a more significant parenting experience and also help you raise exceptional kids who will leave a lasting legacy.

How do we know this?

Sixty-plus combined years of work with children and their families have laid the foundation for the parenting principles that we're going to share with you. More importantly, we've spent the last three decades raising two children of our own, putting our philosophy to the test and discovering the positive results that occur when these nine Straight Line Strategies are intentionally implemented.

Your parenting can and will have a powerful impact—now and in the future—as you bring up the next generation. **Straight Lines for Parents: 9 Strategies for Raising Exceptional Kids** *is designed to be your personal navigational system.*

We are acutely aware that many of these concepts aren't based on our knowledge and experience alone; they are built upon Biblical principles that we learned along life's journey. And while we intend to share many of our own experiences with you, we give ultimate thanks to a gracious God who helped us overcome our own shortcomings in order to move the next generation on to bigger, better, and more exceptional experiences. We are confident that by using these Straight Line Strategies we're going to share, your parenting can and will have a powerful impact—now and in the future—as you bring up the next generation.

Straight Lines for Parents: 9 Strategies for Raising Exceptional Kids is designed to be your personal navigational system that will assist you each and every day moving forward. Some of the Straight Line Strategies we discuss will enhance those you're already implementing, while others may be new concepts that you never considered before. They are simple, straightforward, and meant to strengthen all aspects of your parenting skill sets. We believe you can raise exceptional kids, and there's no better time to start this parenting journey than right now!

Acknowledgements

First and foremost, we are grateful to God for His blessings over the years. He, and He alone, is worthy of any praise we might receive for our achievements in life. Most of all, we are thankful for the hope the Lord gives us—hope for today and for all of eternity!

We are appreciative of our parents who cared for us, guided us, and provided for us during our formative years. They were our first teachers in this parenting process. We love you.

Many other parents supported us during those early, and sometimes scary, days of raising our own children. We'd like to express our gratitude to the many educators who laid the foundation of our careers in Theology, Psychology, and Education. Those mentors added to the diversity and depth of our parenting, as did the years that followed working with children and adults in our professions.

Finally, we would be remiss if we didn't thank our children, Ryan and Jared, who gave us many of the greatest joys of our lives as we raised them into adulthood. Thank you both for allowing us the freedom to practice our parenting skills over the years, and for forgiving us when we weren't perfect at them. We love you more than words on a page could possibly express, and we're extremely proud of the exceptional men you've become!

*This book is dedicated to our sons, Ryan and Jared.
Because of you, we've been on a marvelous journey—
one we look forward to continuing with you in the future!*

Chapter 1

Straight Lines are Intentional

Strategy #1: Raising motivated, inspirational kids that exceed expectations is a direct result of moms and dads who are intentional about following specific "Straight Lines" throughout the parenting process.

One of the most amazing lessons we ever learned about parenting came to us by way of a class called "Puppy Kindergarten." Seriously—we're not kidding! On a cool Saturday morning, we stood with several other proud "parents" of new canines as a trainer explained the basics about raising great dogs. We listened intently, and when the instructor reached the section about the positive results we'd experience based on our intentional efforts and follow-through, something clicked.

We looked down at the little brown bundle lounging on the grass at our feet. She starred back at us, chocolate eyes gleaming, almost begging for some kind of instruction. That's when we realized that everything she was to become would be up to us, not her. If we fed her well, our puppy would probably grow to be a healthy adult. If we trained her, she'd learn the rules. And if we followed through with appropriate rewards and consequences, Jazzmine would have a better chance to make good choices all throughout her lifetime. By the way, it's over fourteen years later, and she's still going strong!

We never expected we'd receive such a profound lesson on parenting, too: *Exceptional kids are a direct result of what we do as parents!*

Let's pause a moment to explain what we mean by "exceptional." What we're talking about here is raising children who will be motivated about life and will live it to its full potential! These are the kind of kids who are curious, caring, and competent, and they will strive to become the best that they can be with their God-given talents and abilities. They tend to exceed expectations, including our own high expectations for them! These boys and girls will become inspirational men and women who will change the world in powerful, positive ways.

> *Exceptional kids are a direct result of what we do as parents!*

What we *aren't* talking about is trying to raise your children to be like our kids, or the kids next door, or the kids from that neighborhood across town. Instead, your goal as the parent is to become an expert in your child—finding out what makes him or her tick, then building on those natural strengths and weaknesses to help your boy or girl become the best that he or she can possibly be. Our ultimate responsibility as parents is to develop our children's physical, intellectual, spiritual, and emotional well-being to their optimum, personal potential.

> *Your goal as the parent is to become an expert in your child.*

This process involves becoming exceptional parents, and that's exactly why you are on this journey right now. No matter where you are in the parenting process, if you want to have great kids—exceptional kids—you're the most important part of the equation! If you use specific strategies designed to reap maximum results, the possibilities are endless! If you choose to do less or little, then expect less or little in return. Why? Because children, like puppies, can't rear themselves, and neither of them will achieve excellence without *regular* and *consistent* input from their caretakers.

> *Our ultimate responsibility as parents is to develop our children's physical, intellectual, spiritual, and emotional well-being to their optimum, personal potential.*

Those seem like two fairly ordinary words. *Regular*: something that happens on a routine basis. *Consistent*: an orderliness, steadiness, and dependability in the process. In other words, this isn't a haphazard, fly-by-the-seat-of-your-pants kind of parenting.

Regular and consistent are what Straight Lines are all about, and that's exactly where we'd like to start your first lesson for raising exceptional kids.

Straight Lines: Markers for Successful Living

Much of our work with corporations through our firm, LEADon, has been founded on "Straight Line Strategies." We believe that Straight Lines are more than guidelines for good living; they are actually boundaries that give personal purpose and focus. They help define roles and responsibilities, whether in families, businesses, or communities. They also direct men, women, and children through the ups, downs, and curves along life's journey by offering direction that encourages positive, forward momentum.

> *If you want to have great kids—exceptional kids—you're the most important part of the equation!*

Clearly-defined boundaries delineate what is right, good, healthy, purposeful, and rewarding. These significant aspects to successful living involve character, morals, values, and ideals. They aid in good-decision making for individuals, families, and society in general.

> *This isn't a haphazard, fly-by-the-seat-of-your-pants kind of parenting.*

Socrates said centuries ago that you won't know a line is crooked until you put a straight one next to it. He couldn't have been more spot on if he were alive today! We live in an era when many guidelines are being put into question. While some values are becoming blurred, other traditional standards are being shifted, muddled, and erased altogether. What's even more disconcerting is that many people are less and less willing to speak up for Straight Lines. Many fear being labeled anything from prudish to prejudice.

> *We believe that Straight Lines are more than guidelines for good living; they are actually boundaries that give personal purpose and focus.*

The best Straight Lines we will ever discover have already been laid out for us in the Bible. God gave His guidelines for healthy, happy, and successful living long ago because His primary desire is take care of His children. Since the beginning of time, our Creator knew how His creation would operate at peak performance, so the Lord *intentionally* shared His instructions about how we should live. This is that owner's manual we all need! But God is a gentleman. He won't force us to read His Word or follow it. That choice—like so many in life—is entirely ours.

From the beginning of the Bible, God records His Straight Line Strategies for great living. He reinforced these throughout Scripture with stories of real people, and real parents, like us (we'll cover much more on Faith in the next chapter as we look at this critical aspect of raising exceptional kids).

Learning about the Lord's Straight Line Strategies will always yield better results than trying to figure everything out on our own, or even worse, going with what modern culture suggests is right! After Moses had died, the Lord reminded the people about His simple, straightforward guidelines for living a wonderful life:

> *Socrates said centuries ago that you won't know a line is crooked until you put a straight one next to it.*

"*Keep this Book of the Law always on your lips; meditate on it day and night, so that you may be careful to do everything written in it. Then you will be prosperous and successful. Have I not commanded you? Be strong and courageous. Do not be afraid; do not be discouraged, for the LORD your God will be with you wherever you go*" (Joshua 1:8–9).

What are the consequences of choosing wisely and following the instructions of the Creator of the Universe? Prosperity and success! We often think of prosperity in terms of monetary rewards, but the term literally means to grow, thrive, and flourish in everything we do. Who wouldn't want this for their lives, and for their children's lives?

> *But God is a gentleman. He won't force us to read His Word or follow it. That choice—like so many in life—is entirely ours.*

Reinforcing Straight Line Strategies

Not far from our home, some new "HOV" lanes opened onto the freeway. This "High Occupancy Vehicle" section of roadway was several years in the making, and its major purpose was to ease the commute for travelers, especially during peak

> *Learning about the Lord's Straight Line Strategies will always yield better results than trying to figure everything out on our own.*

traffic times in our congested section of southern California.

The problem is the entrance to the HOV lanes is rather scary. Not only does the lane exiting the freeway run alongside the entrance, but neither one is very well marked, either. There's always a concern that we might turn into the wrong lane, or that some car that's made that same mistake (which has happened on more than one occasion) may be coming right at us! So, we always slow down, take an extra look at the signage and painted lines, and then turn onto the correct portion of highway.

Isn't life like this sometimes, too? Many pathways aren't as clearly marked as we'd like them to be, and sometimes the choices that lie before us can be a bit daunting! When the stakes are higher, the intensity of good decision-making really sets in. We don't want to be hit head-on by anything, especially when it's completely avoidable.

> *We often think of prosperity in terms of monetary rewards, but the term literally means to grow, thrive, and flourish in everything we do.*

That's why pursuing the Lord's guidance for our lives makes so much sense. If God has already laid the groundwork for a smooth trip, why try something else? If His markers and Straight Lines are already in place, why wouldn't we follow them? Many people in today's society believe this kind of thinking is old-fashioned, out-of-date, or just plain oppressive. One person even told us that our desire to live up to God's standards was "simply the Puritan Police talking to you!" He thought we needed to get with the program and move into the twenty-first century where standards are more like suggestions. Many people today don't even think about defining any Straight Lines!

The problem is that when these time-tested Straight Lines for success vanish, everything is a free-for-all. When ethics and morals are disregarded, men, women, and children have less to live up to. When values collapse, so do societies. If you don't believe us, just do some research to discover what happened to the Romans who once ruled the entire civilized world.

History is replete with lessons about the benefits of living with specific standards—what we call Straight Lines. In these post-modern times, we can certainly reap the rewards of many Straight Lines that exist, whether some people like them or not. In fact, let's look at this from another driving analogy. Whether you commute to work, school, or the grocery store, your drive could be disastrous without straight lines. These include the streets and markers along your journey as well as the rules of the road that keep you and your fellow travelers safe. If someone decides to break a rule—or maybe ignore it temporarily—then drifts into your lane, what happens? A scary moment at best; a catastrophe at worst!

> *When ethics and morals are disregarded, men, women, and children have less to live up to.*

> *History is replete with lessons about the benefits of living with specific standards—what we call Straight Lines.*

Parenting can be just as clear-cut as driving down a well-marked roadway, yet this important role has taken a lot of shots lately. In fact, the boundary lines have become blurry for many present-day parents. We're going to strive to re-emphasize those healthy boundaries for you, hopefully reinforcing some of the strategies you're already using and encouraging you to try new ones that will improve your parenting experience.

Learning how to parent on principles is a lot like a major freeway renovation. It may be messy at first, with lots of dust and old debris that need to be cleared away. The process may seem slow and tedious some days, but before you know it, new lanes of thought will open up. And, before long, you will find yourself on a new, smoother path toward principle-based, Straight Line parenting.

This strategic, Straight Line approach will be a work in progress. You get to learn, and so do your kids! They desperately need standards to live up to during the busy and sometimes bewildering days of childhood and adolescence. And the skill sets you teach them now will not only help them become exceptional kids, but they'll also assist them in growing into outstanding adults who can leave a lasting legacy.

> *God's ultimate goal for the parenting process is to raise up the next generation of children to live for Him.*

God's ultimate goal for the parenting process is to raise up the next generation of children to live for Him. In Deuteronomy 6, we find these words of admonition:

"*These commandments that I give you today are to be on your hearts. Impress them on your children. Talk about them when you sit at home and when you walk along the road, when you lie down and when you get up*" (verses 6–7).

Notice that this is an on-going process of teaching and learning. You've got to learn God's principles so you can pass them on, and you are the one who is responsible for instructing your children. This process must be regular and consistent, and you must be intentional in all of your efforts.

> *Our Straight Lines are based upon what we call the* **Three Pillars of Parenting: Faith, Family, and Education.**

All of our Straight Lines are based upon what we call the Three Pillars of Parenting: *Faith, Family, and Education.* These pillars will be reinforced again and again in the pages ahead. The specific strategies we are going to share are simple and straightforward, and you will be able to immediately put them into practice. As you'll soon discover, these specific Straight Line Strategies will improve your parenting skill sets, and they'll also profoundly impact the experiences you have with your children. Remember, none of this will happen by chance. Exceptional parenting, like raising exceptional kids, is an intentional process.

> *Exceptional parenting, like raising exceptional kids, is an intentional process.*

Intentional Begins with "I"

When we bought our last car and drove it off the lot, we were handed a huge owner's manual, several smaller guides, and a complete DVD packet on proper automobile maintenance. But we are still amazed that there isn't some kind of guidebook or manual that we receive when we leave the hospital with our child. What first-time parents haven't thought at some point: "Are they really going to let us leave with this baby? Do they know how inexperienced we are?" We had more instructions for our four-wheel drive than we did the newest member of our family!

> *Notice that the word intentional begins with "I."*

Instead, most of us exit the hospital with our baby, a basket of goodies, and maybe a few flyers on breastfeeding and umbilical cord care. That's it!

So, it's our responsibility to get up-to-speed on the process of exceptional parenting. And that's exactly why we wrote *Straight Lines for Parents*. We wished we had a resource like this when we began the parenting process. It would have been great to have more ideas about how to discipline correctly, sort out educational needs, and survive the turbulent middle-school years. Sure, we received advice from family and friends, but even observing a good parent doesn't ensure you will become one. You've got to intentionally work at it—every day, all day.

> *God is intentional, too! He promises to instruct us, teach us, and give us direction and purpose. The Lord is an involved parent, lovingly watching over us all along life's journey.*

There's no doubt some of you had less-than-adequate parental role models. Over the years in our counseling clinic, we have had hundreds of individuals and couples come in to work on issues that were directly related to poor, neglectful, and even abusive "caregivers" during their developmental years. These sad, damaging experiences impacted their lives dramatically, including their ability to interact with their own children.

> *Those who reach the pinnacle of success think, plan, study, practice, and even dream about their goals! Can you say the same about being—or becoming—an exceptional parent?*

Let us add an important piece of professional advice: *If the words in the previous paragraph ring a familiar bell for you, and you have not yet sought counseling to directly address these concerns, then we highly recommend that you do so in conjunction with reading this book. The lessons on parenting in the chapters ahead will be greatly enhanced if you take time to deal with issues that are interfering with your ability to parent your kids properly.*

We strongly contend that success in life is all about being intentional. Notice that the word intentional begins with *"I."*

This means that *I* must be the one who makes the effort. *I* am the parent. *I* should make changes when needed. And *I* won't blame him, her, them, or you for anything that is my responsibility.

If I'm a single parent, then I am the one who will have to put these principles into practice. If I have a spouse, he or she can read along, too, and then *we* will each have the opportunity to implement these Straight Line Strategies. Maybe your spouse won't be completely on board with this Straight Line process. That's okay—you can do the work that you need to do for your children and family. Hopefully, he or she will see the positive results of your efforts and join in this powerful process soon.

One of our favorite verses is Psalm 32:8, which reads: *"I will instruct you and teach you in the way you should go; I will counsel you with my loving eye on you."* God is intentional, too! He promises to instruct us, teach us, and give us direction and purpose. The Lord is an involved parent, lovingly watching over us all along life's journey. We especially want to pass this incredible lesson to our children.

The parenting process is timeless. Living with intentionality is a 24/7, all-through-your-life kind of experience. Think of it like an athlete, singer, musician, or artist. Those who

> ***Parenting is truly a higher calling!***

want to be highly skilled in their respective professions work at it. Sure, they may have a greater degree of talent that God gave them compared to us, but whatever that gifting may be, it won't get any better without effort. Those who reach the pinnacle of success think, plan, study, practice, and even dream about their goals! Can you say the same about being—or becoming—an exceptional parent?

If not, here's your chance to establish this new goal and take action in order to achieve it. There's nothing of greater importance that you could accomplish in life! Parenting is truly a higher calling! God has given you the gift of a child for a season, and He wants you to follow His example to become the most outstanding parent possible. When you set this as your primary parenting goal, your efforts can't help but encourage your children to become motivated, inspirational kids who exceed expectations.

My Straight Line NAV System

This "navigational tool" is designed to enhance parenting skills at various developmental stages. Think about ways that you can implement these strategies in your own family.

Birth–5: This age level needs love, love, and more love! But they also need to have structure and a routine. Set up a schedule that works for your family, and stick to it as much as possible.

6–12: Kids at this age should be thoroughly aware of rewards and consequences. Have regular family meetings so you can discuss your expectations as parents, and be sure to give plenty of praise and rewards for positive results and good decision-making.

13–20+: As children move through the life cycle, they change from totally self-centered, "concrete" thinkers to more abstract processors who can understand right versus wrong. Our parenting style must adjust with them; we have to encourage conversations about good behavior, choices, rewards and consequences. This assures their "ownership" in the process and prepares them to enter adulthood successfully!

Chapter 2

It's All About Faith

Strategy #2: Faith is pivotal to developing exceptional kids. Parents need to build their lives on the Lord's principles so that these can be taught to and "caught" by their children.

Almost as soon as our oldest son began talking, we discovered that he often had some kind of question rolling around in his mind. In fact, the phrase "I have a question" has become a funny family memory—especially when he would raise his toddler-sized index finger, tilt his head to one side, and utter the familiar phrase. To be honest, there were some days when we had to say, "Okay Ryan, one more question, and then we're taking a break!"

Yet we also share with parents a profound question that came to us unexpectedly from Ryan's inquisitive mind:

"Daddy, are you God?"

As you might imagine, the silence after that query was scintillating. We looked at one another and smiled, thinking simultaneously: *If he only knew how wrong he was!*

> *Our children learn as much about God from watching us as they do from what we talk about or try to teach them!*

As humorous as it seemed to us, Ryan was quite serious. In his four-year-old mind, Dad must be like God. After all, he is big and powerful and knows a lot—just like the Lord we'd been teaching him about.

That's when the critical message of that moment became crystal clear: *our children learn as much about God from watching us as they do from what we talk about or try to teach them!*

Needless to say, as parents this was a *wow!* moment. Neither of us would ever claim to resemble God, though we strive to live by His principles every day. And the Lord uses our role as "parent" to directly reflect Himself! Our children will get glimpses of God as they see us interact with one another and others in our world. They will come to understand what grace, forgiveness, patience, faith, and love are all about as they observe us putting these values into practice.

> *The most significant aspect of life you can pass on to your children is faith.*

After raising two children into adulthood, we're here to tell you that *the most significant aspect of life you can pass on to your children is faith.* Faith is the foundation for everything that's important, now and for all eternity. And when our kids have this eternal perspective, they will live in the present very differently from most of their peers. Why? *Because our kids will understand that what they do today and tomorrow matters forever!* Their faith will help guide them, correct them, and encourage them long after we have been called home to Heaven. Perhaps not too surprisingly, the parenting process can be one of the greatest tools God will use in our lives to bring us closer to Him too (we highly recommend reading Gary Thomas' book, *Sacred*

> *Adam and Eve's first task included having children!*

Parenting; more details can be found on it, and other great reads, in our Resources section).

So, how do you begin this crucial parenting process? Let's start from the very beginning.

In the Beginning

In the initial book of the Bible, we find our Heavenly Father creating the "first family." Adam and Eve were brought together to complete one another, and soon after, children entered the picture. Actually, the original commands that the Creator gave can be found at the beginning of Genesis:

> **Sin had begun its slippery-slope effect.**

"So God created mankind in his own image, in the image of God he created them; male and female he created them. God blessed them and said to them, 'Be fruitful and increase in number; fill the earth and subdue it. Rule over the fish in the sea and the birds in the sky and over every living creature that moves on the ground'" (Genesis 1:27–28).

That's right, Adam and Eve's first task included having children! They were to "be fruitful" and "increase in number." As they did so, they would literally start to fill the earth, and those family members would help them in caring for the land and creatures they'd been asked to oversee.

But, as you may already know, this original family soon had struggles of its own because of the consequences of sin in what had become a fallen world. Their oldest children, Cain and Abel, brought separate and very different offerings to the Lord, and when Abel's was accepted and his was rejected, Cain grew angry. This anger festered, and eventually Cain killed his brother. As a result, God told him to leave his family, never to return again.

> **He made His design for faith and how to pass it on to the next generation perfectly clear.**

Sin had begun its slippery-slope effect. From Adam and Eve's one act of disobedience with the forbidden fruit, the next generation plunged into outright rebellion against their Creator and His rules for healthy, significant living. And, just like today, the pain multiplied like the proverbial pebble in the pond. Everyone suffered. Division, despair, and even death impacted the entire family.

> *Notice that the Lord's plan for success is extremely simple:* **follow His instructions.** *And the results are equally straightforward:* **you and your children will enjoy long life.**

Yet God, in His graciousness, began the healing process as only He can. Adam and Eve soon had another son, Seth. In Scripture, we find an interesting verse that reveals Adam and Eve may have become more intentional in their parenting efforts, specifically sharing about the special relationship they had with the Lord. Let's look at what happened in Seth's generation: *"Seth also had a son, and he named him Enosh. At that time, people began to call on the name of the LORD" (Genesis 4:26).*

Faith in God suddenly became a noticeable factor. "At that time" men, women, and children started reaching out to the Lord for relationship. It wasn't a given anymore that they'd get an evening stroll in the garden with God like Adam and Eve had years before. Sin had changed things, but they still had the opportunity to be close to their Creator.

> *The procedure for building faith is* **regular, consistent,** *and* **intentional.**

Apparently this intentionality in teaching faith continued for many generations, for we find that Enosh's great, great-grandson, Enoch, was extremely connected to God, so much so that he didn't die a normal death: *"Enoch walked faithfully with God; then he was no more, because God took him away" (Genesis 5:24).* A few generations later, another faithful descendant came along. Noah's devotion to the Lord allowed his family to be spared from the worldwide flood. They would go on to repopulate the Earth when the waters receded thanks to Noah's faithfulness (see Genesis 6–9).

Of course, there were problems in these families, too, and for all the generations that were to follow. But the overall theme we discover in the Bible is that those who obey the Lord's instructions experience a fulfilling life—not free from difficulty, but certainly less impacted by the despair and destruction sin naturally brings in its wake. And God didn't make this concept too difficult to grasp. Indeed, He made His design for faith and how to pass it on to the next generation perfectly clear.

Let's look at the instructions the Lord asked Moses to pass on to the children of Israel in the book of Deuteronomy:

"These are the commands, decrees and laws the LORD your God directed me to teach you to observe in the land that you are crossing the Jordan to possess, so that you, your children and their children after them may fear the LORD your God as long as you live by keeping all his decrees and commands that I give you, and so that you may enjoy long life" (Deuteronomy 6:1–2).

> **Faith is also our own personal North Star that the Lord allows us to use as our navigation system through life.**

Notice that the Lord's plan for success is extremely simple: *follow His instructions.* And the results are equally straightforward: *you and your children will enjoy long life.* In equation form, the plan might look like this:

Obeying God = A Long, Significant Life

Who doesn't desire these results? What loving parent wouldn't want their children to have this kind of blessing, too?

God also asked Moses to share one other detail that would allow this equation to work most effectively, so he continued explaining with these verses:

> *As exceptional parents, our goal is to pass on the importance of faith to our children.*

"Love the LORD your God with all your heart and with all your soul and with all your strength. These commandments that I give you today are to be on your hearts. Impress them on your children. Talk about them when you sit at home and when you walk along the road, when you lie down and when you get up" (Deuteronomy 6:5–7).

How should this formula for optimal living be passed along to the next generation?

1. The parents were to love God with everything their hearts, souls, and strength could give.
2. The Lord's principles were to be thought about and acted upon, regularly and consistently, by the parents.
3. Parents were to *intentionally* talk about faith with their children—at home, on the road, at bedtime, and when they got up.

So, the more detailed version of our formula would look like this:

Obeying God + Loving & Living for Him + Teaching the Children = A Long, Significant Life

Talk about a *wow!* moment for those early followers of God. He offered them the simplest solution for enjoying life to its fullest: *faith!* Their love for the Lord would translate into long life, and by living a life of faith and teaching about it, their kids would get it, too! Notice this formula includes some of the strategic "Straight Lines" we've been sharing with you:

- Faith involves Family (where faith is to be shared first) and Education (the Bible uses the words "impress upon" and "talk about them" as active descriptors of the teaching process).
- The procedure for building faith is *regular, consistent,* and *intentional* (according to these verses, it's a 24/7 process).

So, now that you've got God's original plan for successful living, let's see how you can specifically impact your kids through faith.

Faith is Caught *and* Taught

Faith is often defined as a belief, devotion, or trust in God. It is all of these things, yet it's so much more! Faith is also our own personal North Star that the Lord allows us to use as our navigation system through life. It serves as a filter through which everything in life can be sifted, allowing the good to be adopted and the bad to be discarded. Faith is that firm foundation that everything else in life can be built upon.

People sometimes call things relating to faith by other names. Values, morals, character, and even boundaries are all related to our faith. And individuals who don't want to recognize God also experience degrees of faith in their everyday lives because these same North Star principles rule our universe. What they refuse to credit God with, they often take credit for themselves, or they attribute it to other aspects in life. For instance, they thank "Mother Nature" for good weather, and "the Fates" for

> *Faith development must be intentional.*

helping them avoid an accident. Some will even say things like, "Thank heavens my kids are doing okay" when they don't claim to believe in Heaven at all!

As exceptional parents, our goal is to pass on the importance of faith to our children. Not a secular faith or a general "Sure, I believe there is a God" kind of faith. Instead, we want our children to learn about a real, interpersonal, loving Lord who has an amazing, eternal plan for their lives!

> *Faith is* **demonstrated by** *the parents, and* **experienced by** *the children.*

This kind of faith development must be intentional. If you simply hope it will happen, you will probably be sadly disappointed down the road. And if you don't do anything, you certainly shouldn't expect positive results.

Several years ago, we had a discussion with a friend who had some experience with organized religion but had decided it wasn't for him. He explained how he wanted his children to know *about* God, but he wouldn't force "religion" on them. When we asked if he planned on taking this same course of inactivity regarding their knowledge of reading, writing, and mathematics, he looked at us as if we had lost our minds. "Of course not!" he retorted.

"Well, why not?" we asked in return, "After all, can't your kids catch onto those concepts the same way you hope they're going to 'get' faith?"

He quickly understood our point, and a lively discussion about intentionality in parenting—especially in regard to faith—continued throughout the course of that evening.

Early on in Scripture, God reiterated the importance of passing on His teaching to the next generation, but He also pointed out how this process should begin:

"Now, Israel, hear the decrees and laws I am about to teach you. Follow them so that you may live and may go in and take

possession of the land the LORD, the God of your ancestors, is giving you" (Deuteronomy 4:1).

The members of the older generation were to hear God's instructions, and then *they* were to follow them! Their faithful obedience to His guidelines would be the first step in living the abundant life the Lord had planned for them.

This daily, repeated effort is the critical cornerstone of the faith-building process. As Dr. James Dobson explains, children learn more about the Lord by watching what we do as opposed to listening to what we say. In other words, faith is *demonstrated by* the parents, and *experienced by* the children. We like to call this Faith in Action.

Think about how many things in life you learned by watching, observing, and experiencing, as opposed to simply hearing or reading about them. Look at the concept of driving again: we've all been through the process of reading the DMV manual or sitting in a Driver's Education course. Sure, the rules of the road are explained. Yes, we get images in our mind of what it must be like in the driver's seat, traveling down a roadway with other drivers around us. But until we are actually seated behind that steering wheel with the engine running as we motor down the highway, we don't totally "get it," do we?

So much of life is like this! Whether it's cooking, gardening, home repair, computer work, or interpersonal relationships, humans finally understand the full dynamics of any given situation only when they're knee-deep in it!

> *We're not saying that teaching them isn't important—it is. But first and foremost,* **live your faith!** *St. Francis of Assisi is often credited with having said, "Preach the Gospel at all times, and if necessary, use words." St Francis knew that men, women, and children learn best by seeing a living example.*

Instruction manuals are fine, but life experience beats them out every time.

We like the story of the Apostle Paul's apprentice, Timothy. The young man became a strong witness for the Christian faith, but how did his faith begin? As Paul retells it, *"I am reminded of your sincere faith, which first lived in your grandmother Lois and in your mother Eunice and, I am persuaded, now lives in you also"* (II Timothy 1:5). Timothy had a legacy of faith in his family. In fact, the apostle describes the foundation as a faith that "lived" in his grandmother and mother, so it became alive in him. Timothy learned because of Faith in Action!

> One of the most dangerous paths that parents can travel down: complacency.

This is exactly what we want to encourage you to do with your faith. Live it! Let your kids see you read the Word, pray, treat others around you well, reach out to the poor and needy, and, most of all, love and care for them.

We're not saying that teaching them isn't important—it is. But first and foremost, live your faith! St. Francis of Assisi is often credited with having said, "Preach the Gospel at all times, and if necessary, use words." St Francis knew that men, women, and children learn best by seeing a living example. This reality is exactly why Ryan got the idea that his daddy might be God. He had seen something that resembled what we'd been talking to him about, and he wanted to know more.

> *The Lord also makes it clear that the consequences for not following His Straight Line Strategies will always lead to difficulty and pain.*

Through a mom and dad's great and godly example, kids will naturally pick up the elements of faith. But, as we said earlier, we also should be intentional about teaching the Lord's truths. Here is a reminder from chapter four of Deuteronomy:

"Only be careful, and watch yourselves closely so that you do not forget the things your eyes have seen or let them fade from your heart as long as you live. Teach them to your children and to their children after them" (4:9).

The older generation has the responsibility of teaching the younger generation godly truths and principles. We are not supposed to let our faith fade away, not ever! This means a regular, consistent, and intentional effort regarding our Faith in Action. (As you will notice in our Resources section, we value Dr. Dobson's devotion to the parenting process and his outstanding books on the topic).

Warning: Do Not Enter!

We would be remiss if we failed to mention one of the most dangerous paths that parents can travel down: complacency. We touched on this concept earlier when we talked about Adam and Eve. Had they gotten so used to the fact that they had such easy access to their Heavenly Father that they failed to pass on His principles to their first two children? If that was the case, they

> *Faith must be actively passed on. Real faith. Intentional faith.*

quickly turned things around so that Seth and his generation "got it," for they were the ones who began to call on the name of the Lord.

If it was easy to forget about faithful living then, no wonder we have so many problems today! Perhaps that's why God gives us many examples in Scripture about how to keep the faith ourselves and how to pass faithful living to our children. The Lord also makes it clear that the consequences for *not* following His Straight Line Strategies will always lead to difficulty and pain. Perhaps there's no better story that emphasizes this point than that of Eli and his sons.

For forty years, Eli was a priest in Israel, but he allowed corruption to enter his household by way of his two sons, Phinehas and Hophni. The first description we find of these young men is in I Samuel 2:12: *"Eli's sons were scoundrels; they had no regard for the LORD."*

> We are not called to be our children's friends. God gave us the responsibility of being parents, and that means digging in, standing firm, and speaking the truth as soon as the circumstances require it.

Can you imagine if this is how your children were commonly known by people in your community? What had Phinehas and Hophni been doing to deserve this reputation? Despite being servants of God, they totally ignored His guidelines for administering their duties by taking more of the offering people gave to the Lord than was allotted to the priestly family. Verse 17 actually states: *"This sin of the young men was very great in the LORD's sight, for they were treating the LORD's offering with contempt."*

Where was Eli while all this is going on? Sadly, Scripture reveals a parental absence until one day, Eli couldn't ignore matters any more. Look at what else his sons had been doing:

"Now Eli, who was very old, heard about everything his sons were doing to all Israel and how they slept with the women who served at the entrance to the tent of meeting. So he said to them, 'Why do you do such things? I hear from all the people about these wicked deeds of yours. No, my sons; the report I hear spreading among the LORD's people is not good. If one person sins against another, God may mediate for the offender; but if anyone sins against the LORD, who will intercede for them?'" (I Samuel 22–25a).

These young priests were not only stealing from God, but they were also philandering with women at the very entrance to the place of worship. And notice that Eli "heard" about these things. Why wasn't he aware of this situation earlier? Why was he so absent from his sons' lives that he had to get information from others about what they were doing?

You might be thinking, "Well, at least he did eventually talk to them. That's better than nothing, right?" Wrong! This kind of outright sin and rebellion warranted more than a good talking-to. And notice how Eli had to explain to them that they hadn't just sinned against those around them (and it appears "all the people" knew what was going on); he had to talk to them about how they were sinning against the Lord Himself. Shouldn't these adult men have understood this basic principle of faithful living at this point in their lives?

> *No matter what stage of the parenting process you are in, you can recommit to Him, admitting your failures and asking for His forgiveness.*

How did these young priests respond to their father? *"His sons, however, did not listen to their father's rebuke, for it was the LORD's will to put them to death" (I Samuel 2:25b).* The Lord had enough of their flagrant disobedience and sinning. He knew their hearts were rotten long before their father "got it." And, as is often the case, the parental failure to pass on a real, faithful relationship with God intensified the consequences. Not only did the sons die, but so did Eli and Phinehas' wife (I Samuel 4). The Lord also ended their family's priestly line of service (I Samuel 2:35–36).

The warning for all parents today should be extremely clear: Faith must be actively passed on. *Real faith. Intentional faith.* We can't just expect that because we go to church, put our kids in Sunday School classes or Christian schools, play Christian music in the car, and so on and so forth, that our children will truly understand what faith in the Lord is all about. We need to live it and breathe it ourselves, and we must share what following God means on a regular, consistent basis.

This also means that when correction is needed, we must correct. We are not called to be our children's friends. God gave us the responsibility of being parents, and that means digging in, standing firm, and speaking the truth as soon as the circumstances require it. Sometimes it's a dirty job, but someone has to parent—and for your kids, that someone is you!

Eli failed to pass on what real faith should be about, and this failure had deadly repercussions. Let this be a warning we don't miss along the parenting journey.

Faith through the Ages

Fortunately, the Lord is long-suffering, with us as well as our children. No matter what stage of the parenting process you are in, you can recommit to Him, admitting your failures and asking for His forgiveness. In addition, you should seek His wisdom and strength for the days ahead, because the enemy will definitely try to distract and discourage you in your efforts to follow the Straight Lines necessary for raising exceptionally faithful children.

> *Our goal as parents should be to clearly lay out the pathway to knowing God. We can only do this if we've traveled down that road ourselves and are very familiar with the markers for faithful living.*

Proverbs 22:6 is an amazing verse for parents, and it serves as an excellent reminder that passing along faith can't begin soon enough: "*Start children off on the way they should go, and even when they are old they will not turn from it.*"

Our goal as parents should be to clearly lay out the pathway to knowing God. We can only do this if we've traveled down that road ourselves and are very familiar with the markers for faithful living. We also need to be aware that each stage of a child's development will require adjustment in our approach to leading and guiding them, just as we adjust other aspects of parenting when a baby becomes a toddler, then a child, an adolescent, and finally a young adult.

So, let's start with the same stages we use in "My Straight Line NAV System" at the end of each chapter:

Birth to 5: Research reveals that young children have a unique sensitivity to spiritual matters. This window of opportunity also narrows over time. So, there's no better time to begin lessons on faith than from the first days you discover you are going to have a baby, adopt a child, or marry someone with kids this age. No doubt some people thought we were strange parents, but we used to talk and sing to our babies *in utero*. The best part was when they kicked back! We told them how much we loved them and God loved them. They heard Christian tunes and godly topics from their earliest days.

> *The bottom line: let faith lessons flow as they grow!*

This stage of development is perfect for you to share about the Lord because your babies and toddlers are spending so much time in your personal care. Without the outside distractions that will come in childhood and adolescence, you can talk about faith and God's principles whenever they seem appropriate. Conversations come up naturally as you spend time in God's creation, teaching them about right and wrong, and saying simple prayers at bedtime for family members and friends. Read them Bible stories from colorful books, and play CDs

> *Kids move from being concrete thinkers to being able to consider topics that are far more abstract.*

while they have quiet time. *The bottom line: let faith lessons flow as they grow!*

> The seeds of Faith, Family, and Education that we'd been planting for years were finally beginning to spring to life—big time!

6 to 12: Some of the best investments we made during this stage of life were books, videotapes (now DVDs), CDs, and other faith-based materials. Our boys spent countless hours absorbing Bible stories and character-building lessons through the multi-media approach their generation came of age experiencing. We had few fights with the kids about watching something questionable on television because they had these other options to choose from.

This is also the beginning of some amazing childhood experiences because kids move from being concrete thinkers to being able to consider topics that are far more abstract. Therefore, discussions about God, Heaven, and eternity can have more depth than when they were two or five. As their minds develop, so will their questions! So it's important for us as parents to stay in the Word so we can share Scripture and godly principles with them, which they're going to become much more curious about.

> This is the beauty of multiple voices all throughout our children's lives!

In addition, other children and the relationships they share with your kids are going to become more important. That's why plugging them into programs at church and other faith-based activities with their peers will not only be fun for them, but will also begin to establish patterns of faithful service you want them to continue in the next stage of development: adolescence!

13 to 20+: While some parents dread the "terrible teen" years, for us, these became some of our best memories of parenting. Why? Partly because the seeds of Faith, Family, and Education that we'd been planting for years were finally beginning to spring to life—big time! We watched as our adolescent boys started to make great choices ("No, mom, I don't want to go to that party.") and become academic and athletic leaders at school. There were also fantastic times spent talking about God's truths with our boys as they started to make faith their own.

These are the years when peers are definitely a huge influence, so be sure to stay in touch with their friends. Have parties at your house that are fun and encourage young people to want to hang out. Take their friends along with you to church, on outings, and even on vacation, if you can. Most of all, be sure that you keep your peer-loving teenagers plugged in at church with other believers.

> *For an exceptional parent raising exceptional kids, this process should begin now, not later.*

Finally, mentors will also be increasingly important as teenagers and young adults move through the natural ups and downs of this stage of the life cycle. So, a great youth pastor is critical, but so are aunts, uncles, grandparents, and family friends who love the Lord and will reinforce faith in your soon-to-be adult. Sometimes, our boys would tell us they understood something we'd been talking about for years, just because "so-and-so" said it.

> *Keep pressing on, each day, every day. Soon you'll begin to see the rewards of your efforts!*

> *Never give up! Never surrender! As exceptional parents, our job will never be finished until the Lord takes us home! It's not just 24/7; it's 365 while we're alive!*

This is the beauty of multiple voices all throughout our children's lives!

The stages of learning about faith are as unique as our children themselves. For an exceptional parent raising exceptional kids, this process should begin now, not later. There's no better time than the present to share concepts about the Lord and how to live faithfully for Him! Even if you haven't done as much as you would have liked in the past, don't get stuck there. Keep pressing on, each day, every day. Soon you'll begin to see the rewards of your efforts!

NEVER GIVE UP! NEVER SURRENDER!

Years ago, we attended a conference and were seated at a table next to a distinguished older woman. During lunch, we discovered that "Dorothy" was in her early eighties, enjoyed traveling, and liked attending faith-based seminars like this one. As we made small talk about a variety of topics, Dorothy shared that she was quite concerned about her son who had fallen away from his faith in the Lord.

> *Parenting is one of biggest challenges we've ever experienced, yet it has also been the most rewarding!*

"But," she added with a big smile on her face, "I know God will bring him back because my husband and I taught him about the Lord years ago. My job is to keep praying!"

We have to tell you, this conversation with Dorothy became yet another *wow!* moment in our parenting journey. As we quickly did a little mental math, we figured her son must be somewhere in his late fifties or early sixties, yet Dorothy was still determined to play a part in his faith experience. She had the attitude that we want to pass on to you: Never give up! *Never surrender!*

As exceptional parents, our job will never be finished until the Lord takes us home! It's not just 24/7; it's 365 while we're alive! Now, some of you may feel you've been working so hard with your kids that it seems like you're on death's doorstep, so let us assure you that you aren't alone in those feelings. Parenting is one of biggest challenges we've ever experienced, yet it has also been the most rewarding! Just when we thought we'd had enough, one of our boys would come up and give us a big hug and ask for forgiveness. We'd be so mad at the mess Jared had made, and then he would smile at us with his adorable "funny face," and we'd burst into tears because we were laughing so hard.

> *Life doesn't get any better—and sometimes any worse—than it does with kids.*

Life doesn't get any better—and sometimes any worse—than it does with kids, and some of the hardest trials we're going to experience will be about our children's faith because we have a powerful enemy who is seeking to destroy them. If he can't have them for eternity, then he's certainly going to try to sidetrack them from living the amazing life the Lord has planned for them. And, of course, he wants to rob our joy in the process, too.

That's why we can't urge you enough to take this Straight Line Strategy to heart. Faith matters—first and foremost. We cannot compromise or get complacent because there's too much at stake. So keep going. Don't give up! Live out your faith each and every day, and be sure you're teaching what you know about the Lord to the precious children He's placed in your faithful care.

> *Take this Straight Line Strategy to heart. Faith matters—first and foremost.*

My Straight Line NAV System

Birth–5: Even *in utero*, our children hear our voices. Start singing songs about faith to them. Talk to your babies and toddlers about how much God loves them. Read Bible stories, and invest in faith-based DVDs that you can watch together.

6–12: Children at this age love to learn, so be sure to include lots of faith-based materials in their collection of toys, games, music, and movies. Keep involved as a family at church, no matter how busy life gets. Take time to pray every single night together, and let them ask questions during this quiet time when they aren't so distracted by the demands of the day.

13–20+: Peers are essential to teens and young adults, so encourage social events with other believers and at church whenever possible. Make your home a gathering place for these events, too!

Chapter 3

Family Matters

*Strategy #3: Developing your family unit begins with Relational Equity. This is **the** one equity that children will not stray from as they journey through life.*

We'd like to start this chapter with a confession: *we didn't parent with the purpose of our children liking us.* Of course, we *hoped* they would. Yet, as parents, our job wasn't to be liked. Our parental role and responsibilities did not revolve around being our children's friends. In fact, some aspects of the "parenting profession" don't lend themselves toward friendship at all, especially from our kids' perspectives.

But a recent series of text, voicemail, and email messages have revealed that our endeavors as parents striving to raise exceptional kids are finally bringing in some awesome dividends. It all started when our son and his wife asked us to come for a visit. They had recently moved, and they wanted us to see their new place. We explained that our professional obligations were pressing, and we weren't sure when we could squeeze in the long drive and weekend visit. That's when this young couple became more insistent.

"Can't wait for you to come out and see our new place," one text message read. That was followed by an email with hints about the loft and the guest room awaiting us. After a few weeks passed, and we hadn't yet confirmed a date, the phone calls started: "When are you coming for a visit? We miss you!"

That's when we parents finally got it: Our kids wanted to spend time with us. What were we thinking? Of course we were going!

Needless to say, we blocked out time in our schedules that very day because this is exactly what we'd hoped for years ago—that all of the hard work we put in when our kids were two and ten and fifteen would pay off down the road. In fact, we're just now discovering that we will be able to have a lifelong friendship with our children.

> *After building that strong foundation of Faith, you can help your children grow and develop in the safe, secure environment of Family that you're creating.*

Yet compare this to a scene a dozen years earlier when we had been told we were probably the worst parents in the world, just because we'd disciplined the same son and had sent him to his room for a time out. This comment was just one of many. We were also told that we were awful, we were blowing it, we weren't like so-and-so's parents, they'd need therapy because of us, and so on.

But we kept going anyway, believing that raising our children to become great human beings was far more important than them liking us at that moment. We also knew that if we made our family our first priority, way above everything else we may have wanted or hoped for or dreamed of, the benefits down the road would be far better than any temporary achievement or experience.

In other words, we intentionally chose to put our family first.

Did we have to give some things up along this parenting journey? You bet! We had to turn down speaking engagements, travel opportunities, and nights on the town with friends. And, need we mention that financial resources were allocated to entirely different funds than before we had children?

This idea is the next Straight Line we want to pass on to you as you continue along this expedition of great parenting. After building that strong foundation of Faith (Chapter 2), you can help your children grow and develop in the safe, secure environment of Family that you're creating. To begin this process, let's talk about some of the fundamental principles about family.

THE BASICS OF FAMILY

You've probably figured out that we feel very strongly about faith as the foundation for everything we do in life. Sure, people can go through life doing the best they can and hope that everything will work out for the good. But why do this on your own when the manual for healthy, significant living has already been written and is ready for your daily use? Why would you ignore the guidelines God has already given in Scripture when they are right at your fingertips?

And this is certainly true when it comes to understanding the basics of what family should look like, too. To get started, why don't we study what God says in Genesis:

> *Exceptional children come from homes with a mother and father who love each other, are committed to one another, and are striving to create great home environments in which to raise their kids.*

"So God created mankind in his own image, in the image of God he created them; male and female he created them. God blessed them and said to them, 'Be fruitful and increase in number; fill the earth and subdue it. Rule over the fish in the sea and the birds in the sky and over every living creature that moves on the ground'"(Genesis 1:27–28).

In this introduction to God's Creation, we uncover some simple truths:

1. God made both man and woman in His image. This was the original family unit not to be redesigned or redefined.
2. The first couple was asked to "be fruitful and multiply." In other words, they were encouraged to have children.

For those in modern society who question God's original design and wonder if there can be "alternative plans" for marriage and parenting, we need only to look at the next chapter of Genesis for clarification:

"The man said, 'This is now bone of my bones and flesh of my flesh; she shall be called "woman," for she was taken out of man.' That is why a man leaves his father and mother and is united to his wife, and they become one flesh" (Genesis 2:23–24).

> ***A healthy parenting experience is always preferable to a traditional, yet pathological family experience.***

God specifically made Eve for Adam. The two of them were then united in a sacred bond which would join them in a special relationship. This "first couple" was then urged to have children so they could begin to experience all of the blessings God had planned for them.

As your authors, we have the responsibility to share with you this essential strategy that the Creator initiated. The most meaningful, exceptional family unit will consist of:

1. A man and a woman as husband and wife (heterosexual).
2. A monogamous relationship.
3. A lifelong, marital union built upon faith and faithful relationship.

Interestingly, research supports that this design for the family unit is the *optimal pathway* for children to become successful.

Not too surprisingly, exceptional children come from homes with a mother and father who love each other, are committed to one another, and are striving to create great home environments in which to raise their kids. We have observed similar results in our professional careers. After almost thirty years in counseling and classroom settings, we can often identify those children who are members of well-balanced family units and those who aren't, sometimes within just an hour of getting to know them.

> *God's optimum design for family includes a mom, a dad, and kids.*

Now, this doesn't mean that exceptional children can't come from blended families or single parent families. Many do! In fact, a healthy parenting experience is *always* preferable to a traditional, yet pathological family experience. And if you know that your family is unhealthy—whatever the circumstances you find yourself in as a parent—then seek help from a mentor, pastor, or professional sooner rather than later. This is not only vital for you, but it is also critical for your children.

Despite these directives in Scripture, as well as current research, we're still often asked: Does this mean that exceptional children, or even good children, can't be raised in other types of family units?

Absolutely not! We've seen some of the kindest, savviest, and successful children come out of single parent homes, blended families, and even family environments where grandparents, aunts and uncles, and family friends have stepped in to assume the parenting role. But God's *optimum design* for family includes a mom, a dad, and kids. That's His truth, not ours. We can't apologize for the Creator's design.

> *Each of us brings blessings and burdens into our marriages, and these combine to become some of the parenting "baggage" we struggle with throughout life.*

With that said, if you have been blessed with the role of parenting, then you must assume the corresponding responsibilities with all of the energy and effort you can muster. After all, the original first family ended up being less than perfect—remember Adam, Eve, and their problem children, Cain and Abel?—yet God stepped in to assist despite their imperfections. And He kept doing so with many of the other families that followed.

LESSONS FROM THE "FIRST FAMILIES"

One of the most essential lessons we can teach our children early on is that, once they come to faith in Christ, they are part of God's family. Just like the first family, God made us in His image—that is, exceptional creations of an omniscient and omnipotent Maker.

This also means that children represent their God each and every day of their lives, just like we do. Kids also are representatives of your own family no matter where they are or what they are doing. Some friends of ours like to remind their children, "When you leave our home, you represent God first, our family next, and then yourselves. So, act accordingly!"

> *Faithful living positively impacts our families. As Faith and Family are strengthened, we will not just survive, we'll all thrive!*

What a great goal for exceptional kids to strive toward. But this isn't always easy in a fallen world, and Scripture is replete with examples of many of the difficulties both parents and their children can face during life's journey.

We have three key points we'd like you to consider as we look at the early parenting experiences of some of God's first families:

1. The parent(s) had a variety of personal flaws.
2. The parent(s) experienced failures while parenting.
3. God blessed parents' faithfulness despite the flaws and failures!

The same can be said of parents today. Each of us brings blessings and burdens into our marriages, and these combine to become some of the parenting "baggage" we struggle with throughout life. This baggage includes experiences from our Family of Origin (the family we came from), and then it is combined to form our Family of Procreation (the one we are currently building). So, in a home with a mom and dad, a natural blend of personalities, experiences, strengths, and weaknesses will impact everything.

Yet the Lord can use our flaws and failures to lead us to become more faithful. We saw what happened to Adam and Eve after the tragic events surrounding their two sons (review Chapter 2). They seem to have made some kind of intentional effort to develop Seth's relationship with God differently than they had with their elder sons (remember, Seth's generation is the one that began to openly call upon the Lord).

Yet only a few generations later, things began to deteriorate. By Noah's time, people on Earth were so degenerate that Scripture actually records these words: *"The LORD saw how great the wickedness of the human race had become on the earth,*

> *The Lord worked out the details in this story, just as He has done in many lives throughout history. But those people still had to live with the consequences of their actions.*

and that every inclination of the thoughts of the human heart was only evil all the time" (Genesis 6:5). God decided to destroy His Creation and start fresh in order to form a beautiful race who called on His name. However, God had mercy on Noah and his entire family, and spared them from the worldwide destruction. Why? Let's find out:

"But Noah found favor in the eyes of the LORD...Noah was a righteous man, blameless among the people of his time, and he walked faithfully with God" (Genesis 6:8, 9b).

> *We are made in God's image, and He wired us with His desire to relate. "Relationships are the center of the universe."*

Noah's faithfulness saved his family! His efforts to live a godly life paid off not only for him, but also for all of his loved ones. Can you imagine if you were in Noah's family? How blessed would you feel to have a father and patriarch who God favored so much?

What an admirable goal for us to try to live up to: Faithful living positively impacts our families. As Faith and Family are strengthened, we will not just survive, we'll all thrive!

But when parents fall away from their faith or fail to follow God's Straight Lines for success, their neglect can't help but impact the family. Let's take a look at another famous family. Abram and Sarai (later the Lord would change their names to Abraham and Sarah) were unable to have children after years of marriage. Sarai became impatient, and, despite the Lord's special promise to the couple, she took matters into her own hands:

"So after Abram had been living in Canaan ten years, Sarai his wife took her Egyptian slave Hagar and gave her to her husband to be his wife. He slept with Hagar, and she conceived. When she knew she was pregnant, she began to despise her mistress. Then Sarai said to Abram, 'You are responsible for the

wrong I am suffering. I put my slave in your arms, and now that she knows she is pregnant, she despises me. May the LORD judge between you and me.' 'Your slave is in your hands,' Abram said. 'Do with her whatever you think best.' Then Sarai mistreated Hagar; so she fled from her" (Genesis 16:3–6).

Talk about flaws and failures. This story is full of them! The original error of impatience was now amplified. Here's a quick breakdown:

1. Abram never said anything against Sarai's plan. His lack of leadership from the very beginning allowed problems to escalate in his family.
2. When Hagar did become pregnant, she began to treat her mistress disrespectfully. As a result, Sarai got angry and then blamed her husband for the situation.
3. Abram once again abdicated his leadership role in their family. He basically said, "Fine, she's your problem. Do what you want."
4. Sarai treated the handmaid so harshly that she ran away. Sarai's simple act of impatience escalated to malicious behavior toward another human being.

What a mess! As the story unfolds, we find God intervening and bringing out the best scenario possible *despite* Abram and Sarai's failures. He did eventually reward the couple's belief in Him with the birth of their son, Isaac, He had promised the two of them, but the entire world still suffers today because these parents strayed from some pretty significant Straight Lines. Isaac's and Ishmael's descendents have never gotten along, and this has caused great pain for all humankind.

> *Relational Equity is the one equity that your children will not stray from!*

Let's take a look at another godly person from Scripture that you might assume should have been an exceptional parent. What about David, who was called "a man after God's own heart" (Acts 13:22)? Surely this shepherd-turned-king became a great parent, right? Wrong!

In his youth, David had been a shepherd boy who loved the Lord. In fact, his deep faith allowed him to slay a mighty giant despite his size, age, and overall inexperience. God specifically chose this young man to become king, replacing Saul who had fallen away from the Lord. Yet David, with all of his wonderful attributes, struggled with parenting. Perhaps he was too busy running his business (the kingdom). Maybe we could blame the multiple marriages and manipulation by the mothers of his kids. But the bottom line was that, despite his deep relationship with the Lord, David did not lead his family well. Here's one story about two of his sons, Absalom and Amnon:

> *Parenting is a never-ending role that offers you a lifetime of responsibilities.*

"Absalom ordered his men, 'Listen! When Amnon is in high spirits from drinking wine and I say to you, "Strike Amnon down," then kill him. Don't be afraid. Haven't I given you this order? Be strong and brave.' So Absalom's men did to Amnon what Absalom had ordered. Then all the king's sons got up, mounted their mules, and fled" (II Samuel 13:28–29).

Here we go again! David's son Absalom killed his own brother. And the reason why delves even deeper into the family problems, including an incestuous relationship Amnon had with Absalom's sister two years earlier. What did their father do when he learned of Amnon's incestuous actions? *"When King David heard all this, he was furious"* (13:21). Scripture records that David got angry, but that was it! No other consequences for Amnon's awful actions are recorded.

Is it any wonder we read that *"Absalom never said a word to Amnon, either good or bad; he hated Amnon because he had disgraced his sister" (II Samuel 13:22)*? The lack of follow-through by their father caused division in his household. As a result, Absalom bided his time and took matters into his own hands. He then had to flee because of his actions, leaving David with the loss of two sons and a disgraced daughter. Absalom later forced David to temporarily abdicate the throne until he was eventually killed by one of the king's men.

Again we discover that the Lord worked out the details in this story, just as He has done in many lives throughout history. But those people still had to live with the consequences of their actions. God gives us numerous examples throughout Scripture of His "Straight Lines" for successful living to avoid such pain, offering us the best Education so we can apply these lessons in Faith as we build and strengthen our Family.

Developing Relational Equity

Perhaps one of the greatest themes in the Bible shows that the Lord is all about relationship. He was the Creator of relationship, and He made it a priority from the beginning of time. God actually walked with Adam and Eve in the beautiful garden He designed. He communicated with them, and He made sure all of their needs were met.

That's why relationships are so important for us. We are made in God's image, and He wired us with His desire to relate. We often say that "relationships are the center of the universe." People long to be loved, accepted, and cared for, and they desire to share their love with others, too.

> *Relating must be regular and consistent. It's strategic and intentional.*

And this relationship development is exactly what Relational Equity is all about. Think about a bank account. When you deposit money, you create equity. As the years go on, if you keep adding to that account, the equity will continue to build and build. This is equally true with all relationships—especially with our children. As we invest in their lives over time, we create a sound equity that they can rely on.

> ***Feelings need to be shared face-to-face.***

So we'd like to give you one of our best golden nuggets when it comes to becoming exceptional parents of exceptional children: Relational Equity is the *one* equity that your children will not stray from! Kids will grow up and be willing to turn their backs on money, power, personality, prestige, position, and a myriad of other tempting things in this world, but they rarely will even think about leaving the relationships their mom and dad have established with them because of the tremendous Relational Equity that's been developed.

Relational Equity begins in the crib and carries into adulthood. Parenting is a never-ending role that offers you a lifetime of responsibilities. While the lessons and experiences evolve over time, your "kids" will still need your parental influence even as adults (we will cover lots more about your life-long impact as parents in Chapter 9).

This Relational Equity is developed with lots and lots of time and effort. Babies, toddlers, children, teenagers, and young adults need to spend time with both their parents. Boys need alone time with dad. They also need quality time with mom. Young boys grow up to be great guys when they get a chance to talk one-on-one with dad and when they interact with their mothers away from everyone else. The same is true for girls. Girls will learn how to be women by watching mom, but they'll also learn how men should treat women by spending time with dad.

Relating must be regular and consistent. It's strategic and intentional. None of these concepts should really surprise us, but it's amazing how easy it is to let opportunities to relate with our children slip by because we get too busy or too preoccupied with life.

A great way to relate with our kids is also another essential aspect of building up the Family. We call it "face time."

THE IMPORTANCE OF FACE TIME

When our youngest son went to college, we thought we'd be able to stay in close contact because of the blessing of cell phones. The trouble was, even though his college was situated in a large city, it had terrible cell coverage! We had many frustrating conversations where the connection would be broken up, so we typically finished up by texting each other.

> *Face time means that all electronic devices are turned off.*

But texts, and emails, are best left for facts, not feelings. Feelings need to be shared face-to-face because then you can "read" one another easier as you see facial expressions, hear tones of voice, and watch body language. The same is true of our interactions with our kids. We've got to be present, and so do they, for real Relational Equity to be developed.

Can you imagine what it would be like to carry on a relationship with your children that only involved text messages or the occasional email? And yet these same blurbs of conversation are often what families are doing when parents ask, "How was your day?" and are content with the typical answer: "Fine." Some parents think they've connected with their kids even with such minimalistic conversations.

"Did you learn anything good at school today?"
"Yeah."
"Do you have any homework?"
"Uh huh."

And that's it. No wonder so many children and teenagers are floundering! And no wonder so many families find themselves in the mess they do.

> *If you don't intentionally build in face time with your elementary, middle, and high school children, it will become harder to do so!*

Face time means that *all* electronic devices are turned off unless you happen to be working together on the computer, playing an electronic game, or some other activity that requires them. No one should be texting during face time, not even the parents! We can't tell you how many moans and groans we got when we asked for the television and phone to be turned off at dinner so we could actually talk to one another—and sometimes those moans and groans came from one of us when our shows were interrupted!

Now, we know that face time is always easier when our children are small because they have to have it. Babies need to be held, cuddled, nurtured, fed, and sung to. Toddlers want to play, bounce on you, snuggle while you read, and follow you around wherever you go. As children enter and move through the elementary, middle school, and high school years, they become more independent. This developmental process is healthy and part of God's plan to prepare them for adulthood, but parents sometimes become preoccupied or complacent during this season of life since their children can do more and more on their own.

> *Sometimes that meant we, the parents, needed to learn how to ask much better questions. As exceptional parents, we must stay involved and be interested in our kids' areas of gifting and interests.*

Unfortunately, this developmental progression can begin a slow divide between parents and their children. As kids become more independent, sometimes moms and dads are uncertain about how to connect. Making sure you spend quality time together is essential all throughout your kids' lives—and if you don't *intentionally* build in face time with your elementary, middle, and high school children, it will become harder to do so!

As we already mentioned, some of this face time should be gender specific—moms spending time separately with their daughters and sons, and likewise for dads. However, as much time as possible should be spent together as a family, doing a variety of activities that you all enjoy. Build on strengths and add experiences that will develop weaknesses. Most of all, have fun together! Make your children a priority, and that includes spending time with them face to face.

> *No matter what, make face time a priority in your parenting.*

You've got to ask detailed questions often and regularly. Don't settle for those "uh huh" answers, either. We always required full sentence responses from our sons, no matter what. Sometimes that meant we, the parents, needed to learn how to ask much better questions.

As exceptional parents, we must stay involved and be interested in our kids' areas of gifting and interests, too. You may not be musical, but if your son or daughter is, then go to the recitals, ask them to play for you at home, and show that you're invested in what they care about. We have much more to say about this topic, so stick around for Chapter 6, which reveals how to become an expert in your child.

We can't describe or define what your family's face time is going to look like because every family is different. If one spouse works swing or graveyard shifts and needs to sleep during part of the day, then you may have to adjust your play time and meals to suit the needs of that parent. If your children have activities that require practices in the afternoon and on weekends, then go to them together as a family. Watch, cheer them on, and praise them afterward. Then take time to have a one-on-one talk about the event and what your kids are thinking and feeling.

No matter what, make face time a priority in your parenting. And don't forget that parents need to spend time together, too. This will serve as a great model for your children when they see that you still love and care for one another and that you place one another as top priorities in your family unit.

While all of this may seem exhausting even to think about, the Relational Equity you are developing now will pay off in the long run. The fact that you've made your family a priority will become extremely important when you address one of the more difficult aspects of parenting: discipline!

My Straight Line NAV System

Birth–5: Babies and toddlers need lots of face time, and you can only do this when you keep them the priority. Make sure that mom and dad are both involved during these important years as they are developing their gender identity.

6–12: Find activities that you all enjoy doing together, but also use these years as an opportunity for your kids to learn about their strengths, weaknesses, and gifting. Get them involved in activities that develop their skill sets. Be supportive, even if they choose to pursue activities you don't particularly like!

13–20+: Keep involved with your teenagers and young adults! Sure, friends will be important to them, but so are you. Find fun things to keep doing together, and don't forget that at least one meal a day should include face time with your family!

Chapter 4

Discipline to Self-Disciplined

Strategy #4: Discipline is about passing on good decision-making to the next generation. These skill sets must begin at home, and then they can be honed in real world experiences over time.

"Harder!"

I (Rebecca) couldn't believe what I'd just heard! Our four-year-old son, who'd just received one of very few "swats" he ever had in his young life, looked at me with defiance in his eyes as he spouted the word again.

This wasn't supposed to happen! According to all of the books we had read on parenting, our child should be sorry for his bad behavior after being disciplined. In fact, one of these resources explained that after this short swat, we would then be able to have a great conversation about choices and good behavior.

But after my son's defiance, I didn't want to talk at all. I needed some time to think, maybe even check some of those resource materials again to see what I'd done wrong. But until then, I still had a mouthy child to deal with. I whispered a prayer for guidance, feeling like I'd failed in the disciplining role, and said, "Okay, young man, you're on time out. Go sit on your bed until I come back to get you."

"*No!*" Ryan screamed as if he'd been mortally wounded. "Not a time out. *Nooo!*"

As I closed his bedroom door, a glimmer of hope began to shine. Our little boy hadn't been impacted in the least by a spanking. Instead, he dreaded time alone in his room. This social pre-schooler actually loathed time out!

This led to an important parenting philosophy. We needed to become "experts" in our children. What worked for some kids might not work for ours, and just because a book we'd read said something might be beneficial—well, it might not be the perfect solution for our child.

> *Disciplining your children properly will cause you to become a much more disciplined parent.*

In this case, if we could learn what made Ryan tick, we could help him make better choices all throughout his life. When his brother came along, he confirmed our theory. After trying the same "time out" plan beginning in his toddler years, we discovered that Jared wasn't the least bit affected by this discipline method. He actually loved being alone in his room. He'd sing, talk to his stuffed animals, and get lost in some imaginary world. Yet if we looked at him seriously, then told him in a stern tone that we were disappointed, he broke down in tears. "I'm sorry," he'd whimper, "I'll be better."

These subtle, yet profound, *wow!* moments added evidence to our own parental research that every child is unique, including how they need to be disciplined. This meant we not only had to be more creative as parents, but we also had to become much more self-disciplined ourselves.

THE SELF IN SELF-DISCIPLINE

As you recall, we began this book by telling you how we got an unbelievable lesson about child-rearing by taking our new dog to "puppy kindergarten." Like so many circumstances in life, we discovered that the lessons were much more about what we needed to learn than anyone else's issues. What we'd like to emphasize at the start of this chapter is that disciplining your children properly will cause you to become a much more disciplined parent.

In other words, *correcting your kids in a way that leads them back to good choices requires* you *to think, feel, and act appropriately.* You cannot discipline in anger and not expect an angry, defiant response from your children. Likewise, you can't abdicate your role as a parent and expect kids to pick up the slack and learn self-control on their own.

> *Correcting your kids in a way that leads them back to good choices requires you to think, feel, and act appropriately.*

The message in Proverbs 22:6 gives parents hope that their intentionality in healthy parenting will eventually result in exceptional children, even if the kids wander for awhile: *"Start children off on the way they should go, and even when they are old they will not turn from it."* So, don't be afraid to discipline your kids; their long-term health depends on it!

This is an assertion, not a suggestion. Parents are the ones who must "start children off" properly, with the goal of developing a self-disciplined adult who exceeds expectations. If God had wanted humans to be born knowing intuitively how to grow up and become great adults, He would have created us that way. But He didn't. Instead, He calls actively-engaged parents to raise kids to be self-disciplined as they serve as role models themselves.

One night, we watched an amazing documentary about polar bears in the treacherous regions of the Arctic Circle. A mother bear emerged from her den with a cub. As they wandered around, the pair discovered the unusual camera systems that had been set in place to watch their movements. When the cub got too close to one, the mother gently pushed him behind her with her giant paw, and then gave the sphere-shaped camera a push, sending it rolling down the glacier.

Similar scenes are repeated over and over again in God's creation. When children—whether bear cubs, kittens, chicks, or even baby whales—get close to making a bad decision, parents intervene. Sometimes this intervention even seems a bit rough; for instance, a tigress will pick up her young by their necks and carry them off to safety.

> **When children get close to making a bad decision, parents intervene.**

But that's what exceptional parents do because that's what discipline is all about. Parents intentionally work on training up the children in their care. They teach right from wrong. When dangerous situations do arise, they move their kids out of harm's way. Exceptional parents teach their offspring day-in and day-out so they can be successful in the world around them. Why? Because one day in the future, our children will need to make decisions on their own! To do an extraordinary job of disciplining means we must put "self" on the back burner. We need to learn how to develop respect in our children now so that we can have an amazing relationship with them later. And much of this will require that we learn how to set down Straight Lines and great boundaries they can follow today, as well as every day in their future.

> **Parents intentionally work on training up the children in their care.**

BOUNDARIES BEGIN AT HOME

Over the past three decades, we've had countless opportunities to talk to parents about their children. One theme is consistent in most of these conversations: good parents worry about whether or not they are disciplining their kids correctly.

The great news is that if you wonder if you're doing "discipline" right, then you're already on the right track to doing it better. Exceptional parents evaluate their efforts all throughout the parenting process, which allows us to grow and develop too as we pass great skill sets on to the next generation. Actually, we believe that teaching good decision-making is the foundation for educating our children.

It's important to note that discipline is not an act; it is a learning process for making great choices that's based on relationship. This process of good decision-making is based upon the Three Pillars of Parenting:

1. **Faith**—When people believe in God and understand His principles for great living, they can build upon this foundation for success.

> *Our children will need to make decisions on their own!*

2. **Family**—When individuals make their family a priority, members tend to strive toward keeping that relationship growing.
3. **Education**—When moms and dads intentionally train up their kids, developing their strengths and interests, children will become motivated, curious, competent adults who exceed expectations.

We feel strongly that Faith, Family, and Education are the most critical Straight Lines you can offer your children. Most other aspects of healthy, significant living will usually develop as you build out these areas—both in your life and your children's lives.

The psalmist reminded parents centuries ago that God's principles for living must be intentionally taught *"so the next* generation would know them, even the children yet to be born, and they in turn would tell their children" (Psalm 78:6). The Lord even explained why this training process was necessary two verses later: *"They would not be like their ancestors—a stubborn and rebellious generation, whose hearts were not loyal to God, whose spirits were not faithful to him."*

> **Discipline is not an act; it is a learning process for making great choices that's based on relationship.**

These Straight Line Strategies, therefore, begin in the loving environment that we call Family, which offers examples of balanced discipline and healthy boundaries for all members to observe and follow. Boundaries are important for everyone, but children don't come by them naturally. That's why babies are kept in playpens as they begin to explore their world. As parents, we provide infants with specific items within that setting—objects that we know are safe for them to enjoy. As our babies grow and develop, we talk to them about what is safe and what isn't, and then we put the playpen away so they can start to explore the larger world around them.

> **We feel strongly that Faith, Family, and Education are the most critical Straight Lines you can offer your children.**

These early examples of setting healthy limits are just the beginning of the boundary business. The parenting process is one of constant interaction and training. Nothing can be taken for granted about the "right and wrong" your toddlers may know, so for this period, every electric outlet has a plug and sharp objects are kept away. But we talk about those objects nonetheless, as well as the reminders about making good choices regarding electricity, scissors, and other potentially harmful aspects of life. These important conversations will ebb and flow naturally as part of our developing relationship with our children.

We must set safe, age-appropriate limits for our children, talk about why they are important, and then give our kids opportunities to show us they understand those healthy boundaries before we set new, expanding ones for them.

Are kids always going to stay within these boundaries, especially the first time they are set? Of course not! They are by nature stubborn and rebellious, as the psalmist so poignantly reminds us. But boundaries must be established nonetheless.

As we lovingly set up appropriate boundaries for our children, we must also have conversations about these limits so kids begin to understand how they will impact their lives. Again, these conversations must be age-appropriate. We don't need to tell babies that the safety gate is there to keep them away from the fireplace. But when the toddler heads to the fire, we stop him or her (often over and over again), talk about "hot," and what that means, then put our child back on a course toward making a better choice.

> *Straight Line Strategies begin in the loving environment that we call Family.*

You may be wondering what to do when these boundaries are repeatedly broken, or what to do as your kids get older and you can't put them in a playpen (as much as we might like to some days!) to keep them safe. To answer, let's look at your expanding role in the world of discipline.

Learning about Limits

If we could summarize the steps to exceptional discipline, the process would go something like this:

- Parents determine that their ultimate goal for discipline is that their children will become Self-Disciplined.

- Parents establish age-appropriate boundaries with corresponding rewards/consequences.
- Children are offered many opportunities to practice good decision-making skill sets within the established boundaries.
- Parents expand the boundaries as their kids develop and mature, communicating regularly and consistently so that Relational Equity is also enhanced (see Chapter 3).

You've got some important responsibilities to fulfill, but so do your children. You start the process (Proverbs 22:6), then your kids get the chance to make good choices.

We must set safe, age-appropriate limits for our children, talk about why they are important, and then give our kids opportunities to show us they understand those healthy boundaries before we set new, expanding ones for them.

The vision that you want your kids to catch is that their good decisions will lead to great lives! They will be blessed, thriving in a world where others simply try to make it through another day.

And the vision we must catch as parents is how *critical* this Discipline to Self-Discipline process is. You see, your children will make the most important decisions of their lives when you are not around.[1] Think about that. The decision to take drugs or not won't be in your presence. It will be behind the gym at school, at a friend's party, or in their college dorm room. They'll be alone someday with a person of the opposite sex, and you won't be there to give them "the talk." The groundwork for those choices, and so many more, will have been laid (or not laid) years earlier.

---

1. We want to thank Tyler Durman for reinforcing this concept for us. You can find his and other good parenting books in our Resources section.

DISCIPLINE TO SELF-DISCIPLINED

The ability to make good choices will impact their faith in the God who loves them, their efforts to raise a balanced family, and how they process information throughout their lives. Great decision-making skill sets will allow your children to follow all of the Straight Lines in life. And their knowledge about how to choose right over wrong will be something they will intentionally pass on to the next generation, those who are "yet to be born" (Psalm 78:6).

These rights and wrongs, do's and don'ts include many of the basic skills needed for safe, successful living. Every family will have their own versions of house rules, but all faith-based families should have similar guidelines when it comes to the directives God has given in Scripture.

> *Parents determine that their ultimate goal for discipline is that their children will become Self-Disciplined.*

In addition, as you establish limits and boundaries for your kids, you must consider the cognitive and moral developmental stages of each child. If you have a toddler, elementary school child, and middle-schooler, your rules, rewards, and consequences need to be adjusted to each one's understanding of the decision-making process.

Plus, as an expert in your child, you must also think about the individual nuances of each of your kids as you establish limits, set expectations, and develop plans for rewards and consequences. For instance, when we discovered that our sons responded so differently to time outs and spankings, we had to develop our road to Self-Discipline uniquely for each of them. For one, time outs made him think things through, while the other needed a serious conversation and corresponding

> *You've got some important responsibilities to fulfill, but so do your children.*

consequences (not alone time in his room!) when he'd done something wrong.

We'd like to address another important consideration as you begin to establish boundaries: what to do with special needs children. This is an important topic because many parents have boys and girls who are physically, emotionally, or learning disabled. These children still need limits as well as consequences and rewards, but they should be specifically designed to help them become as self-disciplined as possible given their personal strengths and weaknesses. Many resources are available for parents who need assistance in this process, and we would certainly suggest that you talk with a professional to supplement and strengthen your parenting. Often, support groups that can benefit the entire family are available through counseling sources, community services, or churches.

> *Your children will make the most important decisions of their lives when you are not around.*

Finally, realize that the boundary-setting process evolves over time. As much as we joke and say things like, "Wouldn't it be nice if we could just keep them in their cribs forever?" in reality, this would be a sad state of affairs. Kids aren't meant to stay young forever, and, frankly, we don't want to be the parents of babies forever, either, right? For us, we're enjoying one of the best seasons of life with our flourishing young adults. The Relational Equity we spent years developing is paying off big time, and we're loving every minute of it!

> *Every family will have their own versions of house rules.*

Yet we've actually had some people say to us that we are "lucky" to have ended up with two young men who turned out the way they did. Lucky? We can assure you that chance had nothing to do with it! We've seen the results of families that tried to depend on luck in the parenting process. Many of these had a minimalist parenting approach, deciding that, instead of discipline, they'd "let the kids figure it out on their own." Tragically, they are now dealing with grown children with a host of problems that could have been avoided.

We were intentional and took our role as parents seriously. We know these guidelines worked for us and our clients, and we are confident they'll work for you and your children, too. That's why we're so passionate about passing these Straight Line Strategies on to you.

> *The boundary-setting process evolves over time.*

So, don't be afraid to set safe, healthy limits and boundaries for your children. One day you'll be so amazed to discover that you have motivated, curious, caring, competent children who exceed expectations and are inspirational forces in their world!

A Word of Caution

In the midst of this Straight Line approach to discipline, we need to caution you on a few matters. Discipline is not about punishment; it is about consequences for choices. Children need to understand at an early age that they have free will. They can either obey the established rules, or they can disobey and do their own thing. They also must be taught that included in their freedom is responsibility. Good and bad choices have their respective consequences.

> *Chance had nothing to do with it!*

The best place to explain this natural order of consequences is within the life of faith they're developing. The Bible is full of examples of how God blessed those who chose to follow His guidelines, and, while He was patient with those who didn't, God's Word also shows how the corresponding consequences for bad decisions eventually kicked in. And as people who have experienced the results of good and bad choices, we parents can certainly share some of our own examples about how obeying rules ended up benefitting us, and when disobedience caused more problems than we realized. (Remember to share what is age-appropriate; some of our past problems may need to be kept in the vault until kids can understand and learn from those mistakes).

> *Don't be afraid to set safe, healthy limits and boundaries for your children.*

So, the bottom line for discipline isn't just a "spare the rod, spoil the child" mentality. While sometimes a firmer form of discipline may be necessary (especially when the circumstances are dangerous), we recommend a process whereby you set up established rules, talk about the importance of following them, and clearly share the consequences (good and bad) of choices. In other words, keep lines of communication open! Discuss the good choices, and reward your kids accordingly. Talk through bad decisions, then ask your child to tell you what the family's predetermined consequences are for that poor choice before following-through with that accountability process!

> *Catch kids being good, and reward them accordingly!*

Finally, bullying children into "self-discipline" will never work. We recently heard a mom threaten her toddler in the middle of a grocery store: "If you do that again, I'm going to smack you so hard, you'll regret it." The boy naturally broke down in tears, and those around the mom were stunned. She had just threatened her son for the minor offense of touching something tempting that was right in front of him! What will happen as he gets older, bigger and stronger? Will they then fight and brawl? And what are the chances that this little one will grow up to repeat those same words—and maybe even act on them?

This is exactly why discipline cannot be about punishment. The process leading to Self-Discipline should include conversations that continually point to choices and their respective consequences. It's that simple! The difficult part is that parents must be intentional in this effort and consistent in the follow-through/accountability process.

THE TRUTH ABOUT CONSEQUENCES

As you develop a method of discipline that works best for you and your individual children, it's important that you think about the corresponding rewards and consequences you will implement when those good and bad decisions are made. We can tell you from the outset that rewarding good behavior is the most positive way to inspire kids to behave exceptionally. In other words, catch kids being good, and reward them accordingly!

Rewards need to vary from intangible to tangible.

Why is this true? Because positive reinforcement of the "good" will strengthen that memory within your child, making it much more likely that he or she will want to do something good again in the future. The opposite effect occurs when kids are abusively chastised, belittled, or humiliated. Negative memories will stick, and often attached to them will be thoughts of unhappiness, defiance, or outright rebellion. None of those responses foster Relational Equity, nor will they lend themselves to wanting to be more Self-Disciplined.

Of course we're bribing them! We want to encourage them to make the best decisions possible!

Rewards need to vary from intangible (such as words of praise) to tangible (like stickers on a chart). The goal is for children to eventually need fewer and fewer external rewards because they will do lots of self-praise. Sometimes a simple statement like, "Ashley, I really like the way you cleaned your room today. It looks amazing!" is all that's needed. At other times, you may want to take your kids out for ice cream, letting them know exactly what they've done to earn the reward they're receiving.

> *Instead, children need rules with corresponding rewards and consequences.*

Over the years some parents have asked us if we aren't bribing our children with rewards. Our answer: *Of course we're bribing them! We want to encourage them to make the best decisions possible!* After all, what adult doesn't like a reward at the end of the day? Who doesn't want a Starbucks coffee or praise from someone who appreciates what we've done?

But this "bribery" has a methodology to it. As parents reward good behavior, the ultimate desire is for kids to eventually get to the point where they praise their own efforts. Just as most adults don't need a "good job" every time they've accomplished something, little by little, children will simply feel good about doing the right thing.

> *One of the standard policies we recommend for all families is to use "The Conversation" as part of the discipline process.*

Of course, you also must establish consequences for bad behavior or broken rules. Can you imagine what life would be like in your family if you ignored all bad behavior, waiting for a good decision to be made so you could reward your child? Chaos would soon reign in your home and your kids' lives. Instead, children need rules with corresponding rewards and consequences. That's just the way all humans roll.

As adults, when we're caught speeding, we get a ticket and a corresponding fine. If we do so repeatedly, there are even heftier consequences, and possibly the loss of the right to drive at all. The reward for making a good choice is that we keep our freedom to use the roadways around us. Without these boundaries and consequences to keep us accountable, think of the mess our roads would be!

Like boundaries and limits, consequences must be age-appropriate. They also must be implemented *intentionally* and *consistently*. If you establish a rule for your kids, and it is broken, the consequence should also be applied as quickly as possible. To say to your four- or fourteen-year-old, "Next week you are going to lose your dessert privileges" doesn't benefit either age group. To them, next week seems like an eternity away. But if they lose dessert tonight, or spend time in their rooms, or miss watching their favorite television show, then they'll be far more likely to try the better decision-making route next time.

> **Let them be part of the discussion about what they did and how they can improve.**

One of the standard policies we recommend for all families is to use "The Conversation" as part of the discipline process. You need to talk to your kids about why rules are established and how they are going to be respected (expectations), what happens if they aren't followed (consequences), and what kinds of benefits you have in mind for great behavior and signs of Self-Discipline (rewards). The Conversation also takes place when a rule has been violated. This is a time when you have a face-to-face meeting with your young offender, you go through the rationale of the rules again, and you let them be part of the discussion about what they did and how they can improve.

Believe us, this conversational method may seem time consuming at first, but it will pay off in the end. Open and honest communication helps develop exceptional kids, and eventually they will "get" the lessons you keep talking about. We used The Conversation so often that our boys reached the point where they'd say, "No, not another conversation! We get it—really, we get it!" Of course, we'd have the talk anyway, but they became less frequent over the years as our kids internalized these valuable lessons about expectations, consequences, and rewards.

THE SCHOLARSHIP

Our final word of advice on the Discipline-to-Self-Discipline process is to establish a "Scholarship" policy with your children. In other words, your children need to understand that they are one hundred percent scholarshipped. Technically, nothing is theirs. Instead, everything is a gift offered to them by you, the parent. As long as they follow the established rules and regulations of the organization offering the scholarship (i.e., parents), then they will continue to enjoy all of the rights and privileges granted.

> *Your children need to understand that they are one hundred percent scholarshipped. Technically, nothing is theirs. Instead, everything is a gift offered to them by you, the parent.*

We have used the Scholarship method with our boys, beginning when they were old enough to grasp the concept (for most children, early in elementary school). We explained quite clearly that they were representatives of the Wilke Family; therefore, they were on the Wilke Family Scholarship. As long as they represented their family well, at home and in the community, and followed the guidelines established by us, then they got to enjoy all of the Wilke privileges. If, however, they made bad choices that in any way impacted our family and its guiding principles, consequences would occur—immediately. "Free agency" was always one bad decision away!

In summary: the Scholarship is granted to worthy individuals who want to be team-players and faithfully uphold the high standards and established expectations of the Family.

The impact of this scholarship concept is most noteworthy as your kids enter adolescence and young adulthood. For instance, our sons knew that just because they were eighteen didn't mean they got to do anything they wanted. They were still on the Wilke Family Scholarship as long as they required financial assistance of any kind, so they needed to continue to make good decisions and abide by the rules (which had been changed to be age-appropriate for young adults) that our family had established.

> *Until your children are capable of taking full responsibility for themselves, they must honorably uphold your family's expectations.*

Until your children are capable of taking full responsibility for themselves, they must honorably uphold your family's expectations. Many parents struggle with establishing healthy boundaries and following through with consequences when limits were ignored, broken, or even scorned. Part of the difficulty for parents is that kids have their own strong wills—and strong sin natures—just like us!

Over the years we've had lots of parents share their dilemmas with discipline problems. For example, one couple wondered what to do when their teenager took off in the car because he was angry and then didn't come back until long after his curfew. Another husband and wife couldn't decide if they should do something about their young-adult who had such bad grades in college that she might need another year to finish her requirements in order to graduate.

> *Our answer has been consistent: revoke the Scholarship!*

Our answer has been consistent: revoke the Scholarship! Whose car is it anyway? If you're paying for it, then it's a scholarshipped item! It's probably time for that child to learn how to carpool again or walk, if need be. If your college student is still getting funding from you to attend school, then it's time for The Conversation about good grades versus getting a job until she figures life out. If your children don't or won't play by the rules of your family's scholarship, then you must respond accordingly. Failing to do so will only harm them, and this inaction will never lead to developing exceptional kids.

> *Over-indulged children often become complacent and entitled, expecting a lot without giving back very much in return.*

As most parents have discovered over the course of life's journey, too much of a good thing usually isn't good. Over-indulged children often become complacent and entitled, expecting a lot without giving back very much in return. This is one hundred and eighty degrees from the goal of raising exceptional kids! If you recognize that your children aren't on the path to becoming Self-Disciplined, then it's time to revamp your disciplining philosophy.

> *You can't expect exceptional kids if you're not willing to be exceptional yourself.*

This may also mean improving your own self-discipline as a parent. It will take time, effort, and energy to get things on the right track, but you can't expect exceptional kids if you're not willing to be exceptional yourself. The Discipline-to-Self-Discipline process is possible for all parents to implement, and for optimal results, you need to begin today.

My Straight Line NAV System

Birth–5: Kids at this age must learn the basics of good and bad, right and wrong, safe and unsafe. Your vigilance is critical for their future Self-Discipline. Discuss with them how your Family and Faith help you make good choices, too. Start a reward chart for every child in your family around 3 or 4 years old (see next section).

6–12: Reward charts can be purchased or easily made, and then posted on the refrigerator for each child to see the expectations (bed made, teeth brushed, homework done, etc.). Place a sticker or check mark as each good behavior is achieved, and then reward according to the system your family has established (include kids in the discussion about what rewards will be used in order to get their buy-in). Start "The Conversation" in order to get your children thinking about how to become more self-disciplined.

13–20+: As your kids get older, help them find ways to praise and reward their own Self-Discipline. Continue The Conversation as needed, but allow them to play more and more of a role in this discussion time. Also, the Scholarship is an important tool to help kids become successful adults.

CHAPTER 5

Relationship as Center of Our Universe

Strategy #5: Learning to relate with God, family, friends, and other people is an essential skill that will help every child experience life in exceptional ways. That's because Relationship is the Center of our Universe!

For many people, one of the biggest fears in parenting is that children will struggle with interpersonal relationships. We are concerned about whether our kids will fit in with peers and classmates. In terms of dealing with adults, we hope they'll be able to interact politely and proficiently. We also hope that our children will learn how to make long-term friends and successfully "do relationship" throughout their lives, including getting married and having a great rapport with their spouses.

Not too surprisingly, kids worry about similar things. In fact, as they approach their teenage years, concerns about interpersonal relationships are among their top fears.

Like you, we know these worries all too well. We remember times when one of our boys would return home

> *Concerns about interpersonal relationships are among their top fears.*

upset, bravely holding back tears, because he'd been excluded from the group of kids playing up the street or at school. Even as they grew older, we were concerned when our sons hadn't been invited to some event or party, though they claimed they'd prefer not to attend. We silently wondered if we'd done something wrong. Maybe we'd missed important lessons about how to build good relationships.

> *Learning how to interact with others is critical.*

Despite these moments of insecurity, when we looked at the bigger picture, we realized that our boys were socially well-balanced and able to relate with others in their world in kind, competent, and even exceptional ways. They were polite to peers and adults. They could carry on conversations with all age groups. Even their school report cards and teacher feedback added further confirmation to our own observations about their growing abilities in relating.

But those social skills didn't come along naturally; they had to be taught. We were intentional about equipping our children with the tools needed to relate well with God and others. We also role-modeled these skill sets, using "teachable moments" in their real life experiences to talk about and encourage positive social interactions.

> *We believe that "Relationship is the Center of our Universe."*

Learning how to interact with others is critical, and it is the next Straight Line Strategy that we'd like to discuss with you, because this ability will make or break the foundation of Faith, Family, and Education that you've been developing. Why? Because we believe that "Relationship is the Center of our Universe."

Since God made us in His image, we are pre-wired for relationship. The Lord loves to interact with us, so we have that same desire to connect. But doing relationship well requires certain skill sets, and these must be intentionally taught to each generation.

So, let's set aside any fears or worries for now and look at some new ways to think about relationship. As you're going to quickly discover, helping your children become exceptional in this area will greatly enhance your ability to relate with others, too.

RELATIONSHIP IN ITS PROPER CONTEXT

Have you ever read a quote that was taken out of context? For instance, someone shares a section from a book that really spoke to them, but when you read it for yourself, their comments are completely different from what the author meant. Or perhaps friends tell you about a terrific scene in a movie, but their description doesn't match the film at all. That's because those snippets they shared didn't reveal the bigger picture.

> *Since God made us in His image, we are pre-wired for relationship.*

Perspective is vital for understanding the full meaning of a situation. This is precisely the problem people face today when they try to raise their children using the latest fads or "culturally relevant" parenting techniques, particularly when it comes to talking about relationships. We cannot even begin to comprehend the process of relating without the Creator being the center of the topic—He *is* the bigger picture!

> *We cannot even begin to comprehend the process of relating without the Creator being the center of the topic—He is the bigger picture!*

God made all humans to be like Him: "*Then God said, 'Let us make mankind in our image, in our likeness,* so that they may rule over the fish in the sea and the birds in the sky, over the livestock and all the wild animals, and over all the creatures that move along the ground'" (Genesis 1:26).

First of all, notice the "us" in this verse. God the Father, God the Son, and God the Holy Spirit were in total fellowship from the very beginning of time. Then they created the first man and woman, in part to have fellowship with them.

> **Since we are made in God's image, humanity has three distinct characteristics. We have a mind to think with, a will to choose with, and emotions to feel with.**

By the way, the Lord did not *need* humans to have relationship. In the verse above, we find that perfect relationship existed in the Trinity—yet He created us anyway!

Since we are made in God's image, humanity has three distinct characteristics. We have a mind to think with, a will to choose with, and emotions to feel with. This is how God relates to us, and this is how we will relate to Him, our family, friends, and others in our world. This relational context is designed by the Lord Himself, and it's the structure that will work best if we want to achieve exceptional relational experiences throughout our lives.

> **In order to implement this crucial Straight Line that leads to healthy, successful, life-long relationships, we must follow the plan already perfected by God.**

Of course, God also gave humans free will, which means we can follow or not follow His guidelines for relational living. Many people choose not to pursue the Lord's perfect plan for interpersonal interactions. Is it any wonder then that so many men, women, and children have a tough time getting along?

In our counseling clinic, we are still taken by surprise when parents who've rejected faith as a foundation for their family come to us in order to "fix" their children. These kinds of parents often don't understand why their kids are rebellious, angry, and acting out. Their boys and girls don't want to follow the rules established by the family, and their interpersonal relationships within and outside the family unit are usually suffering—as Josh MacDowell has been saying for years: rules without relationship breed rebellion. Yet when we share some of the Biblical guidelines that would help put their family back on the right track, some of these moms and dads aren't interested in that kind of solution. They don't want to bring "religion" into the mix, even if it would greatly assist their kids in learning how to relate better.

> *Christianity is unique. It is the only faith where humans cannot reach God by their own effort.*

Parents, we're here to tell you that there's no other way to approach relationship! In order to implement this crucial Straight Line that leads to healthy, successful, life-long relationships, we must follow the plan already perfected by God.

Three Vital Areas Needed to "Relate"

The context to the human story then is God not only created relationship, but He also makes it central to all aspects of life. His design includes three essential areas of interaction:

1. Our relationship with God
2. Our relationship with self
3. Our relationship with others

As we discussed in Chapter 2, Faith is pivotal to people's success in life. How we choose to relate to God (or not) lays the groundwork for a smoother, or rougher, journey through life, especially in terms of our interpersonal interactions.

Interestingly enough, wherever you go around the globe, all people-groups establish values to live by, striving to bridge the gap between ourselves and our "god." Christianity is unique. It is the only faith where humans cannot reach God by their own effort. Instead, the Lord lovingly reaches out to men, women, and children, offering them a plan to live to their fullest potential here on Earth and experience eternal life with Him one day in the future.

As parents, we have been charged with training up the next generation in the ways of this Faith (reflect on Deuteronomy 6 again). This means that from our children's earliest days, we need to help them understand what relationship with God looks like, and that their connection with Him is fundamental for all other relationships in their lives. They also need to know that He gives them freedom to live outside His pre-established Straight Lines, but their relational satisfaction will always fall short of what the Lord had intended for them to experience.

> *From our children's earliest days, we need to help them understand what relationship with God looks like, and that their connection with Him is fundamental for all other relationships in their lives.*

In addition, we must teach children that they are important to God. Since they are made in His image, they are unique and special, different from anyone or anything else in the Universe. Your kids should sense that they are set apart by God to glorify Him: *"Do you not know that your bodies are temples of the Holy Spirit, who is in you, whom you have received from God? You are not your own; you were bought at a price. Therefore honor God with your bodies"* (I Corinthians 6:19–20).

We love the line that says, "God don't make no junk." How could He? Everything a perfect, omniscient, omnipotent Creator makes must have His special seal of approval. As the psalmist realized centuries ago, *"For you created my inmost being; you knit me together in my mother's womb. I praise you because I am fearfully and wonderfully made; your works are wonderful, I know that full well"* (Psalm 139:13–14).

Do your kids understand this truth? Do the choices they make about how to take care of themselves and how to treat others reflect this fact? And do they have great personal confidence and feel special because of how you treat them? These questions, at their very essence, are at the heart of learning how to relate.

> *When children truly believe that they are loved by God and you, then they will be more likely to accept themselves.*

If you're not sure about the answers, then now is your chance to change this situation. Start sharing more about how unique your children are to God. Talk about the specific ways that they are extraordinary to you and to the Lord. Let them feel how much they are loved each and every day, from this day forward.

When children truly believe that they are loved by God and you, then they will be more likely to accept themselves. They'll be far more likely than their peers to have great confidence and become motivated individuals, curious about the world they've been placed in because they know they have a special purpose in life. They will be the kind of kids who are caring and competent, sensing that they can be inspirational in their own way. With this kind of confidence, they will truly be able to care for and relate well with others, too.

> *Your children won't be living in isolation, so they need to be able to interact well with family, friends, teachers, peers, community members, and everyone they meet throughout life.*

These "others" are the third piece of the relational puzzle. Your children won't be living in isolation, so they need to be able to interact well with family, friends, teachers, peers, community members, and everyone they meet throughout life.

> *There's an even more critical reason for teaching our kids how to "do relationship." Simply put: a life of faith requires it!*

As adults, we are aware of what it's like to be in the presence of a pleasant person versus someone who is cranky or cantankerous. Men, women, and children respond better to individuals who are considerate and caring. These people inspire us. We're not only drawn to these kinds of individuals, we tend to want to spend lots of time with them, too. Our lives are elevated by others who personally connect with humanity.

So, as children learn to interact with and care about others, the chances that they'll be surrounded by positive people increases exponentially as well.

But there's an even more critical reason for teaching our kids how to "do relationship." Simply put: a life of faith requires it! When Jesus was confronted by a group of Pharisees who wanted to trap Him into a religious faux pas, they asked Him the following question:

"'Teacher, which is the greatest commandment in the Law?' Jesus replied: 'Love the Lord your God with all your heart and with all your soul and with all your mind. This is the first and greatest commandment. And the second is like it: Love your neighbor as yourself. All the Law and the Prophets hang on these two commandments'" (Matthew 22:36–40).

His first point reinforces the essential Straight Line of faith we discussed in Chapter 2. The second point, however, is a reminder that our love for others must be as great as it is for ourselves.

Let's take a minute to explain a few thoughts related to the topic of caring for ourselves. Since Jesus insists that we love others like we love ourselves, we need to first understand how to care for ourselves the way God does. A love and appreciation of oneself involves two key components: personal confidence and self-respect. In almost every instance, confidence and self-esteem are developed over time in a safe, caring environment. Our homes should be the first place personal confidence and self-respect are encouraged, and parents should be instrumental in building these characteristics in the lives of their children.

> *As your kids move from childhood through young adulthood, they still need to hear from you how much God loves them, how much you love them, and how they need to love and care for themselves and others.*

Dr. James Dobson has always contended that developing good self-esteem should be fundamental in the parenting process. This must begin in infancy and carry on throughout your children's developmental stages (see the Resources section for Dr. Dobson's *The New Hide and Seek: Building Self-Esteem in Your Child*).

But can you truly care for someone else if you don't care for yourself? How can you express love to a family member or friend if you don't have value for who you are as an individual created in God's image? So, we've come full circle with the fundamental principle about relationship: *it starts by loving our awesome Creator God and extends to valuing, appreciating, and caring for ourselves and others.*

Do your children have this foundation for relating? If not, the days, weeks, and months ahead should be filled with intentional effort on your part to develop the core values of personal confidence and self-respect in their lives. If you have been working on these fundamental principles, don't stop!

As your kids move from childhood through young adulthood, they still need to hear from you how much God loves them, how much you love them, and how they need to love and care for themselves and others. They also require regular and consistent reminders about sharing that love with a world that desperately needs it. If we want exceptional kids, the effort must begin with us. And, if we truly want to change the world, there's no better way than one child at a time!

EQ VERSUS. IQ: WHY EMOTIONAL QUOTIENT WINS EVERY TIME

People have written a tremendous amount about the Emotional Quotient (EQ) compared to the Intelligence Quotient (IQ) in individuals, and we've listed some excellent books for you in the Resources section if you're interested in investigating these topics further. What's most important for you to know about your children's EQ is that it tends to offer a slightly greater edge over IQ in the long run.

You may be thinking, "What do they mean by that? I thought a high IQ was always to a person's advantage." Well, that's partially true. IQ is a set indicator that can be measured, and it certainly helps to have a decent level of intelligence in order to perform well in school, in your profession, and in life. However, EQ skill sets can develop over time and only get better and better when intentional effort is exerted. In other words, IQ is fixed; EQ is malleable. So, while our intelligence level may be capped because of genetics, our ability to relate with God, ourselves, and others can grow and develop throughout our life spans.

> *IQ is fixed; EQ is malleable. While our intelligence level may be capped because of genetics, our ability to relate with God, ourselves, and others can grow and develop throughout our life spans.*

In addition, improving your EQ serves to enhance your IQ! We have more people with high IQs than ever before in the world, and yet society appears to be in worse shape. Why? Because we desperately need better EQ skill sets! These skills assist us in our personal and our professional lives. For instance, while we may not have the same IQ as another person applying for the same job, terrific EQ may just be the edge we need to secure the position. Why? Because men and women don't necessarily want to work with smart people. Instead, they prefer to have considerate, trustworthy, optimistic, and hard-working team members.

> *We have more people with high IQs than ever before in the world, and yet society appears to be in worse shape.*

We urge you to help your children reach their fullest potential when it comes to IQ (we'll discuss much more about this in Chapter 6 on Education), but we really want you to focus on ways that you can enhance your kids' relational abilities so they can exceed expectations when it comes to interacting with others in their world.

Just like IQ, some boys and girls are gifted with a greater or lesser ability when it comes to EQ. One of our sons had a natural penchant for relating to others. In fact, in third grade, he had a particularly stern teacher who was nearing retirement. She ran a regimented class, which we quickly experienced ourselves when, as we attended Back-to-School Night, this educator told each parent exactly where she wanted us to sit. But our son came home one fall afternoon and stated, "I'm going to win Mrs. M over this year. It may take me all year, but I'm going to do it!"

> *Just like IQ, some boys and girls are gifted with a greater or lesser ability when it comes to EQ.*

You could tell by the smile on his face and gleam in his eye that he meant it. And, guess what? On the last day of school the following June, he received a giant hug from Mrs. M. When we picked him up from school and he told us what had happened, he was beaming with joy. "See, I told you! I knew I'd win her over!"

But not every child has this kind of initiative, especially when it comes to their interactions with others. They need more intentional guidance from us, which means we've got to step up our own game when it comes to EQ.

> *Your kids will learn what you teach them mostly by watching exactly how you "do relationship."*

So, take a few minutes to reflect on how you interact with people in your world. Are you role-modeling kindness, compassion, service, and positive communication throughout your day? How do you speak to and treat your family members? What about the person at the drive-thru window, or in the grocery store, or at a sporting event? Your kids will learn what you teach them mostly by watching exactly how you "do relationship."

> *The added blessing is that these lessons will naturally carry over to the next generation, too!*

Over the years we have observed people of all ages, from children to young adults to senior citizens. Some of them have been incredibly bright, even brilliant. A few were not only in the upper percentile of IQ, but they'd also attained wealth and notoriety over the course of their lives. Yet the individuals we've known who tended to be the happiest and most well-balanced are those with great emotional skill sets and exceptional abilities to relate with others. Despite IQ and other assets, their EQ made them winners in what really matters.

GREAT RELATIONSHIPS FOR LIFE

Nothing is guaranteed in life, and this is certainly true when it comes to raising children. However, based on our own personal and professional experiences, we can assure you that the chances that your children will have happy, healthy, successful relationships will greatly increase if they learn the art of relationship sooner rather than later.

When you help your kids develop a relationship with their Creator, they will have a faith that will last throughout life and into eternity. Wow! Can it get any better than that?

If you add to this the ability to interact well with family, friends, and others in their world—well, you just gave them more than any silver-spooned, trust-fund baby could ever receive. By *intentionally* assisting your children in the art of relating, they will more than likely have great relationships with most people all throughout their lives.

> *Relational Equity, developed through intentional modeling of EQ skill sets, will also make the parenting experience far more rewarding for you.*

The added blessing is that these lessons will naturally carry over to the next generation, too! Because your children will be as skilled as you at role-modeling those positive interpersonal interactions on a regular, consistent basis, your grandchildren will also benefit from all of your efforts.

> *The energy and effort that it takes to raise exceptional kids can seem daunting, but the dividends are priceless!*

Relational Equity, developed through intentional modeling of EQ skill sets, will also make the parenting experience far more rewarding for you, the parent, as you develop a terrific interpersonal relationship with each of your children. For years, we had glimpses of this relational goal with our children, but now that they are adults, we are really reaping the rewards through the great friendship and fellowship we have with these two, fine men.

To be quite frank, it was not an easy, overnight process. We began talking to our boys from the womb on, letting them know how much they were loved by God and by us. As they grew and developed, we spent countless hours singing, reading stories, and discussing their Creator and how He wanted to have a relationship with them. We also worked at growing in our own relationship with the Lord so we could pass Faith on to our kids. And as for family time, let's just say the scales are still tipped on the side of our efforts, way above any personal or professional wishes or desires. Yet we don't regret any of it. In fact, the energy and effort that it takes to raise exceptional kids can seem daunting, but the dividends are priceless!

So think about this relational Straight Line and how you can follow it as you continue this wonderful, wacky, and sometimes wild adventure we call parenting. Relationship is, in our opinion, the centerpiece of our Universe. It's why we are here, it's the essence of what we're about, and it will last throughout eternity.

My Straight Line NAV System

Birth–5: These are the most critical years for children as they begin to formulate their opinion and sense of "self." Use every opportunity to let them know how special they are to God and to you. You *cannot* love your kids too much!

6–12: As children begin to interact with more and more people, actively work on their interpersonal skill sets. If you see them treat someone well, praise them. If they aren't as kind as they could have been, address it gently. Ask them how they would feel if they'd been treated that way. And *role-model* great relationships for them every day. Also, these are important years to get them involved in acts of service for others.

13–20+: Teenagers and young adults struggle with self-esteem issues, and that's often why they take out their frustrations on others. Find opportunities to build their sense of self-worth through their interests and activities. Surround them with positive, caring people, whether family members or friends. Give them lots of opportunity to serve in their community. Most of all, keep them grounded in their faith so they can develop their relationship with God as well as others.

Chapter 6

Education Develops Exceptional Kids

Strategy #6: Parents' primary focus must be on becoming an expert in their kids. Only then can the educational process make its most powerful impact.

It didn't take long in our parenting journey to discover that we had a lot to learn about raising a child. Then we added another to the mix, and our shortcomings only seemed to multiply. But occasionally, we'd get an epiphany that helped enhance our skill sets, like the following example we learned one night while preparing dinner.

"Mom, I don't want pasta. I don't even like pasta!" our then six-year-old piped up while the noodles were boiling on the stove.

"Well, I like pasta," our other son chimed in, "but I don't want chocolate ice cream for dessert. I've never liked chocolate!"

This began a pre-dinner discussion about all the things one liked and the other didn't, and vice versa. While putting the final touches on dinner, we couldn't help but overhear all of these differences between our two children. Later, we compared notes and came up with more dissimilarities of our own.

One son loved to sleep; the other thought four hours was the perfect amount because he liked to play at two in the morning!

Both boys liked other kids, but one would share his toys while the other didn't really want to. The oldest was neat and tidy, while the youngest preferred a much more "casual" approach in his room. One thrived early at team sports, while the other liked more individual types of athletics.

We wondered: how did these two kids ever come from the same set of parents? And how on earth were we going to be able to teach and help these children develop with those varied likes, dislikes, strengths, and weaknesses?

> *Parents must become experts about each of their children, for then—and only then—will they be able to educate and develop exceptional kids!*

That's when we arrived at another *wow!* moment that helped spark the next Straight Line Strategy in our parenting philosophy: *parents must become* experts *about each of their children, for then—and only then—will they be able to educate and develop exceptional kids!*

It doesn't matter how we were raised, what parenting seminars we've attended, or what great books we've read; parents must figure out exactly who their own children are as individuals. Exceptional parents know what drives and motivates their kids, and they direct them along pathways that will be optimum for their success.

> *Understanding what makes each of your children "tick" will take time, effort, and energy. You will have to give them lots of attention, and you'll need to pay attention!*

This personalized expertise is a fundamental component of the third pillar of parenting: Education. As you have been building out Faith (Chapter 2) and Family (Chapter 3), you have already begun the educational process. With those two key pillars in place, you can then begin to equip your kids with all of the other essential skill sets needed to become motivated, curious, caring, competent, and inspirational human beings who exceed expectations.

Understanding what makes each of your children "tick" will take time, effort, and energy. *You will have to give them lots of attention, and you'll need to pay attention!* Sometimes our boys' and girls' nuances are discovered in quiet moments, like when we pray with them before going to bed. At other times they'll be seen on a grand scale—for instance, when one of them scores a touchdown then dances a celebratory jig, or when another child tries out for the lead in the school musical when you didn't even know he or she liked to sing!

> *We don't need more experts or counselors to help raise exceptional kids; instead, we need more extraordinarily involved parents.*

We don't need more experts or counselors to help raise exceptional kids; instead, we need more extraordinarily involved parents. It's definitely a time-consuming process, but what you're going to discover is far beyond whether or not your kids like pasta or playing piano. You'll learn what their deepest passions are, many of which they will carry with them into adulthood. So, get ready for one of the best parts about parenting: becoming the expert!

BECOMING THE EXPERT IN YOUR CHILD

If Education begins with becoming an expert, then we'd better start this chapter with a simple definition. For our purposes, this expertise means that parents must be "in tune" with their children's physical, emotional, spiritual, and academic strengths and weaknesses.

Let's break those down for you briefly before we continue. Here is what we mean when we're discussing these key areas of development:

Physical: Every child will be gifted with a body that works in extraordinary ways, but like us, they will have their share of challenges. Some will run fast, others will be slow. Certain children will be balanced and coordinated, but there will be those who struggle with even the simplest tasks. Parents must help their children's physical development in every way possible while understanding some genetics will determine their ultimate capabilities.

Emotional: All of us are wired differently when it comes to emotional responses. Even as babies, some children cry easily or are unsettled when their schedule changes. Many boys and girls go with the flow, while others require lots of structure. As parents, you must learn the nuances of each of your children, assisting them to build up those weaker areas in their emotional skill sets so they can become well-adjusted adults one day.

> *Parents must be "in tune" with their children's physical, emotional, spiritual, and academic strengths and weaknesses.*

Spiritual: As we've shared previously, faith is one of the fundamental aspects of a child's development that must be intentionally addressed by parents. God has given each of us a spiritual capability, but like all abilities, it must be developed over time. Staying "in tune" with your children's spiritual development will be critical for their ultimate success and satisfaction.

Academic: While many experts contend that IQ is fixed based upon genetics, even this potential will not be reached without proper educational effort throughout a child's developmental years. School and other learning opportunities will assist in this process, but it is the responsibility of parents to actively participate in the educational development of each of their children (more on this to follow shortly).

It's not enough just to have your kids living under the same roof with you. Don't expect to absorb what they're all about if that's where your "intentionality" ends. This must be a developmental journey that you engage in on a daily basis. As your children grow, so too should your knowledge about them. How are they doing physically? What do their bodies need at this stage in terms of proper nutrition, exercise, and rest? How are they feeling about themselves, their friends, and life in general? What about their spiritual progress? Are they learning about God and faith as is age-appropriate? What are their strengths and weaknesses when it comes to academic abilities? What do they do well? What do they require extra assistance in?

> *This must be a developmental journey that you engage in on a daily basis.*

Notice that we've mentioned strengths and weaknesses. As we'll discuss later when we cover Multiple Intelligences, research shows that everyone has a variety of educational skill sets which can be developed over time. Some of us will be stronger in certain areas—like linguistics—while others may struggle with reading, writing, and communicating. The good news is that even the weaknesses aren't fixed in stone. Our children can grow and develop in all areas, but they need an expert to help them do so.

> *The good news is that even the weaknesses aren't fixed in stone. Our children can grow and develop in all areas, but they need an expert to help them do so.*

And guess who that expert is? That's right—you! Expertise in your children is not the job of schools, churches, clubs, sports, or scouting. These are great supports to the pillar of Education you are developing, but you are the primary caregiver and, therefore, the primary source for all areas of expertise when it comes to your children.

> *You are the primary caregiver and, therefore, the primary source for all areas of expertise when it comes to your children.*

When we talked about discipline in Chapter 4, we discussed how becoming an expert in each of your kids is critical for equipping them with the skills needed to become self-disciplined. At the core of success for this Self-Discipline process is discovering what makes your kids "tick." You get to discover what motivates them and what makes them thrive!

Too many kids in this world are simply surviving. They get up each morning to the television blaring, a "get your own breakfast" mentality, and a "see you later" as they're dropped off at school. When they arrive at home, too often, no one is there to greet them. When a parent arrives, little to no real communication takes place. A "how was your day?"—"fine" exchange doesn't build Relational Equity let alone represent a minimal level of expertise in the life of your child.

> *When you do gather again for family time, take a few minutes to download about your son or daughter's day.*

What does help develop expertise? A sit-down breakfast together, if possible, and certainly all electronic devices off as you start your morning. Talking about the upcoming events of the day sets your children up for success, and so do hugs, kisses, and an "I love you" before anyone runs out the door. When you do gather again for family time, take a few minutes to download about your son or daughter's day. Ask questions that require more than a yes or no response, and follow up by sharing about your day, too. Let them know that relationship is a two-way street—not an interrogation process!

And these interactions are just the tip of the iceberg to finding out who these beautiful creations really are, the ones you've been given charge of for a short season to equip and develop into exceptional kids who will one day be exceptional adults. Notice that it all begins with you, and it definitely starts at home!

Education—Home Schooling at Its Best

Human beings begin the learning process early. In fact, we assert that education actually begins before birth. This means that as babies develop *in utero,* these little ones are growing in every way humanly possible, including in their educational development.

How can this process begin so early? By the way you prepare siblings for the new arrival. By the way that you speak to your yet-to-be-born child. By the environment you and your spouse create and live in, including the nursery where you will bring him or her home. Basically, by everything your family is doing to get ready to raise this new, wonderful boy or girl created in God's image.

> *We assert that education actually begins before birth.*

As we've shared, we talked to our children and sang to them while they were in the womb. The amazing part was that they actually started moving and even kicked back in response! We realized early on that this precious gift of life knew something about what was happening in the outside world.

Then after birth, the fun really begins! From their earliest days, children's eyes watch you intently. They are absorbing everything around them, especially what it means to be human by watching you. From your tone of voice to your facial expressions, they are also learning something about what you already think about them.

This information is absorbed and continues to be processed as they grow and develop. They give you feedback along the way, too: that first smile, the initial sounds they make, and little hands that reach out to discover and make contact with their surroundings.

> *Parents, we're the ones who are called to "impress" the Lord's truths upon our children!*

The start of their educational process is learning from you and from the environment you're developing for them to grow up in. The Lord intended children to learn in this way! He created family first, with the chief objective of giving moms, dads, and children a safe, supportive environment to experience life in. As we've mentioned before, the home setting is the initial training ground for what Family and Faith should look like. Remember theses verses from Deuteronomy?

"These commandments that I give you today are to be on your hearts. Impress them on your children. Talk about them when you sit at home and when you walk along the road, when you lie down and when you get up" (6:6–7).

> *Parents must equip their children with the skill sets they need to live a life of faith, create their own thriving family one day, and keep learning all throughout their journey here on Earth!*

Parents, we're the ones who are called to "impress" the Lord's truths upon our children! Impress—literally meaning "press shape into something," as if you were modeling a piece of lumpy clay into a lovely piece of art.

But this chapter of Deuteronomy includes even more detail on this educational process:

"In the future, when your son asks you, 'What is the meaning of the

stipulations, decrees and laws the LORD our God has commanded you?' tell him: 'We were slaves of Pharaoh in Egypt, but the LORD brought us out of Egypt with a mighty hand. Before our eyes the LORD sent signs and wonders —great and terrible—on Egypt and Pharaoh and his whole household. The LORD commanded us to obey all these decrees and to fear the LORD our God, so that we might always prosper and be kept alive, as is the case today. And if we are careful to obey all this law before the LORD our God, as he has commanded us, that will be our righteousness'" (Deuteronomy 6: 20–25).

> **Parents *are the ones* who must remain the central, driving force in their own children's educational development.**

As children grow older, they will start to formulate questions of their own about Faith, Family, and other vital matters. So God gave guidelines to the parents not only on what to say but also about how to do it. These verses offer several key steps for parents to follow as children become more involved in the learning process:

1. Let kids ask questions!
2. Give them specific, age-appropriate answers.
3. Explain the rationale for learning these lessons, especially the consequences and rewards.

Notice that the Lord *knew* kids would ask questions as they grew up, and they'd want to know more about their world than just the "rules." He didn't say to stifle that cognitive developmental process. Instead, He

> *So, take your role and responsibilities to heart, and home!*

encourages moms and dads to continue the conversation, now at a deeper level. Children aren't to be hushed and told "just do it because I (or God, the Bible, your teacher, Grandpa, the government, etc.) said so." No, the Creator understands that those sweet, adoring babies develop first into concrete thinkers, and then eventually into abstract intellectuals. He gives every child a great mind—and why not, we are made in His image! In this section of Scripture, it's clear the Lord wants parents to take advantage of these teaching opportunities.

> *Our strengths and weaknesses can be addressed during the course of a lifetime.*

This is home schooling at its essence and also at its best: parents equipping their children with the skill sets they need to live a life of faith, create their own thriving family one day, and keep learning all throughout their journey here on Earth!

Now, we don't mean that parents have to do this on their own. As life-long educators, we are advocates of excellent schools, strong sports programs, inclusive community activities, and other family-friendly, supportive opportunities for our children. So, *the role of raising exceptional children will be greatly enhanced through interactions with others and through a variety of experiences during their lives.*

> *Becoming an expert in your children means that you must take responsibility for understanding which areas of Multiple Intelligences they are gifted in already.*

But *parents* are the ones who must remain the central, driving force in their own children's educational development. You are the hub of the wheel, the force that should guide as well as decide what paths your children will take. When your kids' futures are at stake, you simply cannot abdicate this God-given role because the consequences are too drastic.

So, take your role and responsibilities to heart, and home! Think about what ways you can improve your children's education simply by becoming more involved in it yourself. Carve more time out of your day to be "hands-on" with your children—talking, laughing, teaching, praying, playing, and just enjoying being together. As you do so, you'll discover multiple ways that you can truly enhance the value of Education in their lives.

Multiplying Your Child's 'Multiple Intelligences'

Centuries ago, John Adams shared his philosophy of education this way: "There are two types of education…one should teach us how to make a living and the other how to live." In order to accomplish both, parents must discover the strengths and weaknesses in each of their children, and then they must help develop those appropriately as they prepare kids for adulthood. One way to do this is by discovering your child's Multiple Intelligences.

We were introduced to the theory of Multiple Intelligences while working in our respective fields of study. This concept basically confirmed what some parents already know: kids are smart in multiple ways, not just in reading, writing, and arithmetic.

> *Remind your children that they are special to God no matter what gifting they have.*

You can probably attest to the reality of Multiple Intelligences because of your own experiences in life. For example, some individuals are gifted in music, art, dance, gymnastics, or relationships. None of these quite fit into what most of us experienced in school with the three "R's." Yet reading, writing, and arithmetic also are their own kind of gifting.

Dr. Howard Gardner and other researchers decided to study the various types of intelligences observed in children and adults. They compiled a list of eight main categories in which these "gifts" (Multiple Intelligences) align. Dr. Thomas Armstrong then put these into layman's terms for us. He calls the eight areas of Multiple Intelligences:

1. Word Smart (Language)
2. Logic Smart (Mathematics)
3. Body Smart (Bodily-Kinesthetic)
4. Picture Smart (Spatial)
5. Music Smart (Musical)
6. People Smart (Interpersonal skills)
7. Self Smart (Intrapersonal skills)
8. Nature Smart (Environmental Awareness)

The importance of both of these researchers' work has been most evident in today's schools and classrooms, where many educators have adapted curriculum and instruction to address children's various areas of gifting. But as the first and primary educators, we encourage parents to be more informed about these concepts, too (we recommend reading a book by Dr. Gardner or Dr. Armstrong; check the Resources section).

> *How could we possibly do any less for our children?*

Another wonderful aspect about Multiple Intelligences is that boys, girls, men, and women have more than one! In fact, we will often exhibit strengths in several areas. And another exciting discovery in the research done on Multiple Intelligences is that weaknesses can be improved! In fact, our strengths *and* weaknesses can be addressed during the course of a lifetime.

Becoming an expert in your children means that you must take responsibility for understanding which areas of Multiple Intelligences they are gifted in already. Then you must develop those as part of their educational process. Again, this begins at home, but it also includes encouraging those strengths at school, at church, and in the community. Give your kids chances to succeed in these areas of natural ability, and praise them for their achievements regularly and consistently.

As for those areas of weakness, once you've identified them, you can begin to provide opportunities for improvement. Let's say you've noted that your child doesn't seem to have much musical ability; then turn up the music! Your children can listen to different types of music, attend concerts, take lessons, and even go on the Internet to observe musicians in action. If your kids aren't that athletic, then take them out and play ball with them, attend high school, college, or professional games, or have them join a team at the local recreational center (there's often less pressure in this setting, especially when your boy or girl is learning a new sport).

> *He has combined this perfect mix of qualities and given you the reins to take charge, "breed up," and lead them though their developmental years and into adulthood.*

Most of all, remind your children that they are special to God no matter what gifting they have. Share with them the words of Psalm 139:13–14: "*For you created my inmost being; you knit me together in my mother's womb. I praise you because I am fearfully and wonderfully made; your works are wonderful, I know that full well.*"

Each child is created specifically by God, formed to be exactly who they are today! They are wonderfully made by an amazing Creator who has a special plan and purpose for their lives. As parents, we can instill this understanding of their uniqueness like no one else can—more deeply than teachers, pastors, coaches, club coordinators, or other mentors. If you tell your children how exceptional they are, then they will tend to live up to that vision!

Expert parents developing exceptional kids must know the strengths and weaknesses of each of their children. Educating them according to their gifts and building up their weaker areas of Multiple Intelligences will greatly enhance their opportunities for success now and in the future!

"Breed 'Em Up"

Years ago we were privileged to have the renowned preacher, Dr. E.V. Hill, in our home. He shared about his life, especially his family that he adored. As our own two young boys played nearby, Dr. Hill stopped his conversation to watch them for a few minutes. Then he turned to us and said something we'd never forget:

"You've got to breed 'em up."

> *Exceptional parents realize that there are no cookie cutters for children.*

We both looked quizzically at Dr. Hill, and after a few moments passed, then we finally asked, "Dr. Hill, what do you mean?"

"You've got to breed these kids up like racehorses! They can't do it on their own." Then he went on to describe how owners of thoroughbred horses take good care of their expensive animals. They feed them the best foods, and they keep them in the best stables. They are given the right amount of exercise depending upon their age, and they are trained by specialists for the races ahead of them.

Since that time, we've known a few people who've owned horses, and we discovered Dr. Hill was right. The more elite the horse, the better overall care it received. Those owners spared no expense to make sure the creatures in their care were brought up from infancy in the best manner possible so they'd become exceptional adults.

How could we possibly do any less for our children? As Dr. Hill reminded us that day, our goal as parents is to "breed up" our beautiful children to their fullest potential. This is an intentional process—and one that demands regular, consistent attention. Like those phenomenal horses, our children have their own races to run. We are simply called to prepare them for that future God has in store—and enjoy the journey!

Final Thoughts on "Expertise"

All of the Straight Line Strategies that we've been sharing with you are geared toward this prime objective: helping you develop exceptional kids. Your children are unique! God created them with special gifts, interests, desires, and, yes, even weaknesses. He has combined this perfect mix of qualities and given you the reins to take charge, "breed up," and lead them though their developmental years and into adulthood. No one else can do what you're charged to do, and, quite frankly, you shouldn't want anyone else to have that tremendous responsibility.

> *What a calling! What a journey!*

Exceptional parents realize that there are no cookie cutters for children. Instead, mom and dad get the joy and privilege of learning about the nuances of each of their unique children, and then they get to use that knowledge to develop their kids' physical, emotional, spiritual, and academic strengths and weaknesses. This process is Education in its essence, and it is your skill set to master.

In a world as diverse as ours, we need individuals who have technical knowledge, academic abilities, musical and artistic talents, and interpersonal and intrapersonal skill sets. We want kids who know the three "R's," but we should also want them to operate skillfully within their strengths so they'll be happy, thriving, exceptional adults someday.

We believe children today need to be college- or trade school-bound because we live in an era when a high school diploma often isn't enough to move beyond ordinary and reach extraordinary status. In fact, at the time we are writing this book, unemployment is over nine percent, but for those with a college degree, the number is just under four percent. So, encourage your kids to learn, and make Education a value in your family.

Life-long learning is essential to those spiritual matters we've discussed—especially when it comes to healthy, significant living. King Solomon explained the importance of Education this way:

"Let the wise listen and add to their learning, and let the discerning get guidance. Listen, my son, to your father's instruction and do not forsake your mother's teaching. They are a garland to grace your head and a chain to adorn your neck" (Proverbs 1:5, 8–9).

But as children are "listening," we must be teaching! We must become experts about our kids and then use that knowledge when we get up in the morning, as we talk to our kids, while we're fixing meals, and even right before they go to sleep. Then, as they grow and develop, we've got to make adjustments. When they ask questions, we must listen and then give appropriate answers. If our children try something and don't like it, we must help them find something else. And if they do fail at something, we have to be there to offer hugs, acceptance, forgiveness, and more Straight Line Strategies to get them back on track.

What a calling! What a journey! You have the opportunity to venture down the road of learning, step-by-step, with your precious child. You get to teach, guide, quiz, listen, pray, and teach some more—and then watch your children blossom into the exceptional individuals you've been waiting for!

My Straight Line NAV System

Birth–5: Spending lots of time with your kids during this age will allow you to learn their personalities, strengths, weaknesses, wishes, and dreams. Give them lots of opportunities to try new things that are age-appropriate.

6–12: The Multiple Intelligences of your kids should be very visible during the elementary school years. Provide positive experiences that build upon their strengths, and praise their achievements. In weaker areas, offer non-threatening ways to try new things. And if they fail—well, try, try again with something else!

13–20+: Teenagers and young adults are still able to improve in all areas of Multiple Intelligences—as are you. Find activities that you can do together to not only build Relational Equity but also increase strengths and improve weaknesses. Don't forget to keep up the praise! This age group may act like they don't like it, but they relish the kudos as much as adults do!

Chapter 7

Personal Responsibility and Parenting

Strategy #7: Exceptional parents make personal responsibility a value. Demonstrating good judgment and making wise choices are among the most important virtues you can teach your children.

Not long ago we ran into an old friend, and we stood in the late morning sunshine catching up on one another's families. We'd known the couple since college, but, in the past few years, life had gotten busy and we had lost touch. Jake shared that their twins were now in their late twenties and married, and their youngest son was in college studying. After we updated him on our family, Jake said the most amazing thing:

"You know, our kids grow us as much as we help them grow up."

For us, that was another *wow!* moment in the world of parenting. As moms and dads—even as we're working hard to raise exceptional children—the parenting process grows us up too! This is particularly true when it comes to personal responsibility.

For many men and women, becoming a parent for the first time is an awakening on many fronts. The seriousness of this new role settles in quickly, as do the very specific responsibilities that coincide with the gift of a child. In our opinion, no other role will require so much time, energy, and effort, but nothing else this side of Heaven will offer the same kind of rewarding experiences and opportunity for life-long relationship!

Sadly, our culture has currently devolved into one of "entitlement," which certainly adds nothing to the concept of personal responsibility. Instead, an entitled culture actually erodes the accountability process that leads to significant living because individuals begin to believe that they are "owed" something by their mere existence. The notion of earning—whether privileges, opportunities, money, position, or even respect—is devalued. Instead, entitled people believe they deserve these things just because they're here.

> *Sadly, our culture has currently devolved into one of "entitlement."*

Can you imagine how this entitled attitude could negatively impact children? If kids begin to think that they don't have to earn things, then how will they be motivated to work hard? If they start to believe that they should receive the best without having to do much, if anything, in return, then what are the chances they will want to become exceptional?

As we share with individuals in many settings, everyone is born with the opportunity to live to their highest potential in any given situation, but this does not guarantee equal results. In other words, equal effort does not mean equal end products. But all of us can excel when it comes to personal responsibility!

The art of taking ownership for our choices is the glue that binds Faith, Family, and Education together. For instance, when you take personal responsibility for your faith in God, this means that *you* have chosen to follow or obey Him. When it comes to family, *you* have elected to be loyal, supportive, and devoted to each member, and you desire to keep the family unit together. And in terms of education, *you* get to make the choice to achieve at your highest level of potential, and to continue learning through all of life's experiences.

When you have all of the Three Pillars of Parenting in place, the chances for long-term success are much greater than being strong in one pillar but weak in the others, or hoping that you'll be "lucky" when it comes to you and your children's lives. We don't believe in a multiple choice mentality when it comes to Faith, Family, and Education. Exceptional parents *choose* to develop all of these foundational areas for the benefit of everyone in their family unit.

> *Exceptional parents must intentionally desire to teach personal responsibility to kids if they hope to raise children who are motivated, curious, caring, competent, and exceed expectations.*

Given the impact of an increasing entitled attitude in society, the accountability process isn't an easy task, but exceptional parents must intentionally desire to teach personal responsibility to kids if they hope to raise children who are motivated, curious, caring, competent, and exceed expectations.

The concept of personal responsibility as a binding agent for the Three Pillars can be observed best when we compare flourishing family units to those that are just barely making it. When parents don't role-model good judgment and sound choices, children often follow in their footsteps. These moms and dads may very well want their kids to,

> *When parents don't role-model good judgment and sound choices, children often follow in their footsteps.*

"do as I say," but human beings of all ages have a tendency to do as their parents, and others, do!

This tendency to copy what is modeled for us is why we see so many bad patterns of living passed down from generation to generation. Whether it's gambling, greed, promiscuity, unethical behavior, or chemical dependency, these acts of *irresponsibility* don't happen by chance or because a family is "cursed." Rather the role-modeling overrides the rule-making every single time.

> *The role-modeling overrides the rule-making every single time.*

So, parents who want to change the next generation must intentionally strive to do so each and every day. This transformation must begin with mothers and fathers, and then as they role-model good behavior and sound decision-making, children will tend to duplicate what they've observed and experienced.

Now that we've laid down the foundation for personal responsibility, let's expand on this Straight Line that will solidify your exceptional parenting.

VALUES VERSUS PRIORITIES

Personal responsibility must become a "value" in your life. Yes, this means you value it—think it's important—but it also means much, much more. A value is a strongly held virtue or belief. Its importance is so essential that you are willing to fight for, even die for, the truth it represents. Honesty, integrity, and loyalty are some of the character qualities good parents value.

> *Exceptional living is all about values.*

Priorities, on the other hand, are things or circumstances that, while important, often change regularly, even hourly, depending upon the demands of life. Taking a nap isn't something you'd probably choose to fight over, and you certainly wouldn't be willing to lay down your life to get your weekly workouts in!

Getting to work on time is also a priority for most of us, but if one of our children gets sick on the way to school, we wouldn't have any problem calling our employer to say we'll be running late or perhaps not coming in at all because of our child's needs. Why? The *priority* of not being late was superseded by a *value*: taking care of our son or daughter.

Exceptional living is all about values. When we shift our mindset from doing things according to what we consider a "priority" to essential values, the Straight Lines to significant living will make more sense. Faith, Family, and Education are the three core values we've centered our Straight Lines around, and those encompass many areas of your life that—you'd probably agree—you'd die for: your kids, your marriage, your belief in God, and your desire to learn, grow, and develop according to God's calling in your life.

> *Value-driven, principle-based living isn't easy in the current culture that is full of priorities but low on values.*

Value-driven, principle-based living isn't easy in the current culture that is full of priorities but low on values. Yet we desperately need more of this kind of parenting because value-driven parents raise value-driven kids. If we truly want to improve the next generation, we've got to identify what we value—and then let those virtues be our guide throughout life.

We are often asked, "What's the best way to raise great kids?" Our answer is that your children will be exceptional when they have a mom and dad who simultaneously role-model personal responsibility. When ownership is a value to exceptional parents, they strive to make the best decisions possible for themselves and for their families. They also have what we call a "Back Burner" approach to parenting. These parents realize that they're greatly valued in God's eyes, but they don't have to be the center of attention. They're willing to put their desires on the back burner as they make God, their family, and the "breeding up" of their kids the primary focus of their lives.

Now, we have described a mother and father as role-models for personal responsibility. Does this mean that single-parent, divorced, or blended families can't end up with exceptional children? Certainly not, but please recognize that the same process will be more difficult for these families. Why? Once again, it's because the God-given guidelines for raising great kids were laid down for us long ago, and that plan was ideally in the context of a healthy, traditional family striving to follow God's Straight Lines for success.

> *Value-driven parents raise value-driven kids. If we truly want to improve the next generation, we've got to identify what we value—and then let those virtues be our guide throughout life.*

If you feel your circumstances aren't quite measuring up, this is the perfect time to ask for divine assistance in applying God's principles about personal responsibility. He will answer and help you get back on track. God is more than able to meet your needs, offer wisdom, and guide your steps in this incredible parenting journey!

> *Your children will be exceptional when they have a mom and dad who simultaneously role-model personal responsibility.*

Also, spend time considering what you truly value, and even write those virtues down so you can reflect on them as you parent your exceptional kids. You may need assistance from a mentor, pastor, or professional counselor as you set goals to change unhealthy generational patterns and begin a new journey for your family. Finally, don't forget that we have all fallen short of the Straight Lines that God has given humankind to follow, so ask for His grace as you get up, dust yourself off, and take these new steps in the right direction.

Understanding the Good about Good Choices

Making good choices is what those striving to be great parents hope to do, but hoping only goes so far. We have to *want* to have good judgment, and then we've got to *follow through* by making sound decisions.

To be honest, it's a challenge for humans to make excellent choices on a consistent basis, but the benefits of doing so far outweigh the consequences of poor judgment and bad decisions every time. As adults, we've experienced the negative consequences when we've chosen poorly, even in the seemingly simplest of circumstances. We may not like all of the "rules" life has, but we've learned through trial and error that most of them are for our long-term benefit.

> *We have all fallen short of the Straight Lines that God has given humankind to follow.*

Let's return to our driving analogy. Just because we cross a line or go over a designated speed limit, a uniformed officer can pull us over and write a ticket. We then have to pay the fine for that ticket. If we make another poor choice, like putting off paying the fine, we'll have even tougher consequences. Yet even the most law-abiding citizens can become annoyed when they're punished for going "a little bit" too fast, or getting distracted while driving (could it have been the kids making noise in the back seat?).

This struggle with authority, and with taking responsibility for our choices, occurs in so many aspects of our lives. Perhaps this is why Paul, one of God's messengers in the early days of the church, wrote, "*We know that the law is spiritual; but I am* unspiritual, sold as a slave to sin. I do not understand what I do. For what I want to do I do not do, but what I hate I do" (Romans 7:14–15).

Thankfully, our God helps us in this age-old battle of good versus evil, great choices versus bad decisions. A few verses later, Paul added, *"What a wretched man I am! Who will rescue me from this body that is subject to death? Thanks be to God, who delivers me through Jesus Christ our Lord"* (Romans 7:24–25).

> *If we as parents can be transformed, so can our kids! We must set the example first, and then live by that example.*

This means, with God's help, we can overcome our propensity to disregard rules, disobey, and get detoured from His Straight Line Strategies for living. If we as parents can be transformed, so can our kids! We must set the example first, and then live by that example. We should pass on the knowledge that we have about the rewards for good decisions, as well as why they are definitely worth the effort in the long run!

In Galatians 6, we find encouragement as parents about the importance of good decision-making:

"Do not be deceived: God cannot be mocked. A man reaps what he sows. Whoever sows to please their flesh, from the flesh will reap destruction; whoever sows to please the Spirit, from the Spirit will reap eternal life. Let us not become weary in doing good, for at the proper time we will reap a harvest if we do not give up" (6:7–9).

It's a pretty simple Straight Line that the Lord lays out here: if we do what pleases our own selfish wants, desires, and interests, the end results won't be pretty—but when we strive to live according to God's guidelines, blessings are promised!

Some people call this a "blessings and curses" approach to life, but we prefer to call it the Law of Natural Consequences. God isn't out to "get you" when you do wrong, but because of His goodness, there are consequences for not following His guidelines, so that we can learn from our mistakes and change to be ever closer to our goal of great living.

Consequences occur when we make poor choices, and parents must help their kids understand that natural result. There are also plenty of rewards, those good things we'll experience and, most importantly, eternal blessings from our Heavenly Father.

Parents, your job is to understand and live out these Straight Line Strategies! When you do good things, God is pleased. That's what should matter most. And as we make great choices each and every day, our children will have the best role-modeling for how to incorporate good decision-making into their lives, too.

Personal Responsibility 101

When we talk to men and women, we remind them that their parenting role is like a contact sport. In fact, sometimes it's more of a collision sport! Certain days are going to be rough, and sometimes you're going to feel banged up by the battles you must fight in order to be an exceptional parent. But even when you're tired, you still must role-model good decision-making. If you've made a mistake, you need to take ownership. No matter how rude or rotten the other party involved might have been, if you've played a negative role in a scenario, show your kids what it means to take personal responsibility by trying to make the situation right.

> *When we strive to live according to God's guidelines, blessings are promised!*

Learning how to make good choices should start sooner rather than later. From their earliest days, we taught our sons that they didn't have to *be* the best, but they had to *do* their best. We also shared with them that life may not seem fair, yet they were to strive to do the right thing anyway. As soon as they could process the concept, we talked about how they weren't entitled to anything—except to work hard and try to please God in the process.

Some of these lessons on personal responsibility began in the smallest of ways. For instance, we didn't remove things from the coffee table or not hang ornaments on the Christmas tree lower than five feet from the ground just because we had toddlers in the house. We used the word "No," and we meant it. Believe us, children can learn what "No" means early in life, but, just like us, their little hearts and minds will struggle to accept this boundary.

> We taught our sons that they didn't have to be the best, but they had to do their best.

That's when the accountability for personal responsibility has to kick in. When our boys were toddlers and decided to disobey and touch the item on the coffee table or the Christmas tree, they got a firm "No." If they stopped, they were rewarded with words like, "Good job, buddy." When they chose to reach out and touch it again, they got reprimanded more firmly: "No, that wasn't' a good choice!" If they repeated these poor choices, the "Wilke Three Strikes Rule" took effect. They were immediately removed from the area, told what they'd done wrong, and received a timeout in order to think things over. These kind of quick, clear responses are essential for younger children in the concrete-developmental stage of life.

> We used the word "No," and we meant it.

As our kids grew older and developed as more abstract thinkers, The Conversation was added to their consequences. As we mentioned before (see Chapter 4 on Discipline), our kids knew "The Conversation" was coming when they had bad judgment and made poor choices! But these were times to discuss and let them process for themselves what they'd done wrong, what decision would have been better, and what they thought the consequences should be for their poor judgment.

There were also lots of opportunities for praise and rewards following great decisions. This process is much like we've talked about when it comes to discipline, because, after all, taking personal responsibility involves Self-Discipline, too. As your children grow and develop, there will be numerous ways that they can learn about the benefits of making good choices. Some of these opportunities will come naturally through life experiences (we'll talk more about this in Chapter 8), but exceptional parents will have the best chance of passing on this Straight Line Strategy for success as they reward kids for acting in responsible ways.

> *Exceptional parents will have the best chance of passing on this Straight Line Strategy for success as they reward kids for acting in responsible ways.*

Don't get weary in this critical process! We do reap what we sow, and for parents, working hard at raising exceptional kids will eventually pay off. Sure, there will be tough times (that's the collision sport part of parenting), but there will be seasons of great Relational Equity, good family interactions, and tremendous growth in you and your children. Savor all of those golden moments.

When things don't go according to plan, remember that you're living in an imperfect world where things are not always fair. People who parent poorly sometimes have great kids (go figure!), and good things don't always happen to good people. This is also part of the Law of Natural Consequences we discussed earlier. We are living in a fallen world, and a consequence of imperfection is, well, imperfection!

We cannot always correlate personal responsibility with a definite positive outcome, at least, not here on Earth. Yet

> *People who parent poorly sometimes have great kids (go figure!), and good things don't always happen to good people.*

remember the words in Galatians above? *"Whoever sows to please the Spirit, from the Spirit will reap eternal life. Let us not become weary in doing good, for at the proper time we will reap a harvest if we do not give up"* (6:8b–9). The proper time for a reward might not be right now. Perhaps it will be a little later, or a lot later. Maybe your reward won't come until eternity, but God promises you will eventually be rewarded for what you've done.

This kind of personal responsibility is a mindset, and it is truly a paradigm shift from the society in which we live. Yet, if you are willing to intentionally work at making exceptional choices, you will have a much better chance at changing your family history and guiding the next generation down a path that leads to significant, inspirational living.

A Tale of Two Brothers

One of the reasons we love to share stories from Scripture is that the Bible is full of examples essential to good parenting. So, let's start this section by spending a little time looking at the tale of two brothers:

"Isaac prayed to the LORD on behalf of his wife, because she was childless. The LORD answered his prayer, and his wife Rebekah became pregnant. The babies jostled each other within her, and she said, 'Why is this happening to me?' So she went to inquire of the LORD. The LORD said to her, 'Two nations are in your womb, and two peoples from within you will be separated; one people will be stronger than the other, and the older will serve the younger'" (Genesis 25: 21–23).

In the book of Genesis, we find that these two brothers actually began their sibling rivalry in their mother's womb! It was so intense, Rebekah asked God for some guidance, and He let her know in a clear way that these boys would grow up to be very unique.

These differences were observed from birth on: "*The first to come out was red, and his whole body was like a hairy garment; so they named him Esau. After this, his brother came out, with his hand grasping Esau's heel; so he was named Jacob*" (5:25–26a). And, just as we discussed in Chapter 6, their areas of Multiple Intelligences were quite diverse, too: "*The boys grew up, and Esau became a skillful hunter, a man of the open country, while Jacob was content to stay at home among the tents*" (5:27).

> **We cannot always correlate personal responsibility with a definite positive outcome, at least, not here on Earth.**

Esau liked the ruggedness of the outdoors. His brother Jacob, the "heel catcher" (which the Hebrews also used as a term for deception—we'll see the reason why Jacob fits this description later), preferred to stay home and help out there. Sounds like a nice family unit, right?

Well, it certainly had the opportunity to be, but let's take a closer look at what Scripture reveals about the twins' parents: "*Isaac, who had a taste for wild game, loved Esau, but Rebekah loved Jacob*" (5:28).

In one short sentence, God reveals a huge gap in Isaac and Rebekah's parenting. They played favorites, and everyone, including these two boys, knew it. They weren't just teaching their boys that life wasn't fair, they were living it out day by day! And that's not all, after Esau traded his birthright as the first born to Jacob for a bowl of soup, their mother would become part of a plot to have her husband give Jacob the firstborn blessing:

> **The proper time for a reward might not be right now. Perhaps it will be a little later, or a lot later.**

"Then Rebekah took the best clothes of Esau her older son, which she had in the house, and put them on her younger son Jacob. She also covered his hands and the smooth part of his neck with the goatskins. Then she handed to her son Jacob the tasty food and the bread she had made" (Genesis 27:15–17).

> *God reveals a huge gap in Isaac and Rebekah's parenting. They played favorites.*

While there was division in this family (and more that would follow because of the mistrust this dishonesty caused), the bottom line is that the generational problem of deception was continuing right before the children's eyes. In fact, if you know the story of Isaac's parents, Abraham and Sarah had lied years before when they were in Egypt! So, as Rebekah literally clothed her youngest son in a deceiving outfit to fool her blind husband Isaac into giving his blessing, she continued a legacy of bad judgment and poor decision-making in the process.

As is often the case, this unhealthy generational pattern was passed on to Jacob's sons. They sold their brother Joseph (interestingly enough, their father's "favorite") into slavery, and they killed a goat to cover Joseph's clothes in blood so they could tell their father, Jacob, that he had been killed by a ferocious animal (see Genesis 37 for this family's continuing saga).

> *The generational problem of deception was continuing right before the children's eyes.*

You may be thinking right about now, "Hey, wait a minute. God told Rebekah from the beginning that these brothers weren't going to get along. They were destined to have those problems!"

Well, hold that thought. Of course, God, in His omniscience, knows everything that's going to happen, but He didn't tell

Personal Responsibility and Parenting

Rebekah the exact path that would lead her sons to become two different nations of people. Because of His righteous character, it makes sense that He might have had a much better plan for those two boys, and for this family. God's desire wasn't for division (starting with the parents who chose favorites) or deception to be part of this family's history. Like us, however, they had free will—and they chose poorly.

During our careers, we've had numerous parents tell us something like this: "Well, God knew that my son/daughter would turn out like this, so I guess that was His will."

That's when we stop and explain "Yes, God knew what would happen because He understands all things, but that doesn't mean this was His perfect plan for your child! It also doesn't mean that you didn't make choices along the way that resulted in his/her current negative patterns."

> *This unhealthy generational pattern was passed on to Jacob's sons.*

Remember, parents, God's *permission* in free will doesn't mean He will be *pleased* with our choices.

But no matter what has happened in the past, exceptional parents can and will change things right now by getting back on track with God's guidelines for parenting their children.

Take up the "Never Give Up! Never Surrender!" attitude that great parents must have in order to raise exceptional kids. Sure, terrible generational patterns may exist in your family history, but with God's help and your Straight Line parenting skills, this can change. And just because you've struggled or fallen short in your parenting doesn't mean you can't transform into the kind of parent the Lord wants you to be now. You can change! You *must!* This is especially true if you want the next generation to be free from negative patterns that have damaged your family for years.

The Water Buffalo Story

We have a tale about the lack of personal responsibility in our own family that we now refer to as "The Water Buffalo Story." It began when one of our sons lied to us about where he had taken "his" car which was packed full of other guys. On the top of a steep mountain, he blew out a tire on a sharp rock. When the boys tried to fix the truck, it almost rolled over on top of them! Of course, we didn't find any of these details out until twenty-four hours after it happened, when we took the damaged vehicle to a store to replace a thrashed tire.

> *Because of His righteous character, it makes sense that He might have had a much better plan for those two boys, and for this family.*

"Oh my!" the tire repairman said with a shocked look on his face. "What happened? This looks like someone ran over a boulder? I can't believe the car didn't flip over!"

We reflected on the story that our son had told us the night before—how he and his friends had simply driven down a main road in town and hit a rake or something, then heard the tire pop. The teenagers had put on the spare tire, then returned home. We repeated our son's tale to the repairman just as it had been told to us.

> *Take up the "Never Give Up! Never Surrender!" attitude that great parents must have in order to raise exceptional kids.*

He looked at us incredulously and said: "A rake? This looks like your son hit a water buffalo!"

Later, we asked our son if he had told us the entire story, and he looked at us with big, innocent eyes and replied, "Yes." That's when we shared what the man at the tire store had said—and then the truth came pouring out.

"I'm so sorry, I'm so sorry! It was horrible. We could have died! I promise I won't ever drive off road again!"

We could tell he was sorry, and grateful to be alive. But there were consequences to be paid for his poor judgment and lying (which thankfully didn't end up harming himself or others). His driving privileges were revoked for several weeks (which seemed like an eternity to him), and he had to work to pay for the new tire we replaced. He also knew that it would take time to rebuild trust with us, because the lack of responsibility compounded by lying would never be acceptable in our family.

> *Our kids make bad choices just like we do.*

Even though our boys knew this type of scenario wasn't ever supposed to happen, it did. Why? Because our kids make bad choices just like we do. Yet as exceptional parents, we must choose to become better individuals ourselves, and then we must hold our children to the same high standards we've established for our family. Many times we were tired, but we kept going. There were days we wanted to stop this "collision sport" we'd gotten ourselves into, but God gave us the strength to continue trying, because He also helped us recognize the dire consequences that could occur if we abdicated our God-given parenting role.

> *There were days we wanted to stop this "collision sport" we'd gotten ourselves into.*

And after three decades of work with parents and families, we are here to tell you that one of the most important parenting objectives you must have, from your child's first breath to your last one, is to teach personal responsibility. You must intentionally pass on this Straight Line about making wise choices. You should strive daily to role-model how to live responsibly, and you also have to define your values and incorporate them in everyday experiences.

All parenting lessons must include personal responsibility. Why? Because learning to make good choices will keep the Three Pillars of Faith, Family, and Education standing strong! It is the glue that binds these beliefs and virtues, and it will solidify other principles in the lives of your exceptional children.

> *One of the most important parenting objectives you must have, from your child's first breath to your last one, is to teach personal responsibility.*

We understand what a sacrifice taking complete ownership of our lives means, and the time and effort required to pass the Straight Line of personal responsibility to the next generation will be great indeed. But exceptional children who exceed expectations can only develop on this straight-forward path! Remember, the rewards for personal responsibility and good choices are reaped each step of the way, and your children will be able to sow seeds of these exceptional life choices for generations to come.

My Straight Line NAV System

Birth–5: Even in their highchairs, children can learn that they don't spit or throw food. If they choose to do so, there must be consequences. If they decide to act correctly, they should be rewarded. Look for very tangible lessons to practice growing their understanding of personal responsibility.

6–12: At this stage, kids can have great discussions about the good choices they see happening in the world versus poor decisions. This is the time for parents to be teaching lots of stories from Scripture that reinforce lessons about personal responsibility, too. Keep conversations going, and don't neglect to follow-through with rewards and consequences.

13–20+: As kids reach the teenage and young adult stages, they will have numerous opportunities to observe good decision-making and personal responsibility in action. Talk to them about their experiences at school, in the community, and with their friends. Most of all, don't forget to keep role-modeling personal responsibility yourself—it will still have tremendous impact, especially during these busy years of growth and development.

CHAPTER 8

Life Experience and Your Exceptional Kids

Strategy #8: Parents must actively provide opportunities for their children to learn through daily, real-life experiences.

The Little League game played out like a script from a Disney movie. The two teams that had vied all season for first place now met on the field for the final championship. One team's manager had the reputation of playing dirty, a "win at all costs" kind of guy. The other manager was a new dad in the neighborhood, and the other fathers/managers didn't like the fact he'd had so much success during his first year on their turf.

As for the kids, they just wanted to play ball, and hopefully win so they could go celebrate at the local pizza place. So the umpire started the game, with the underdogs (yep, those managed by the nice guy) falling quickly behind. By the time the last inning arrived, only a grand slam home run would win the game, which seemed unlikely since the slightly overweight boy who hadn't really hit all season was up to bat.

And that's exactly when the magic happened. "Mighty Joe," as he would from that day forward be known, swung his bat and somehow connected with the fast pitch that came straight at him. From the loud crack of the bat, everyone in the crowd knew something amazing was about to happen. Joe's ball sailed far beyond the outfield boundary—far beyond where anyone had hit all season! He followed the three boys on base to home plate for the walk-off win!

People were on their feet cheering, clapping, even crying. The winning team and their beloved manager jumped up and down in a circle on the baseball diamond. Never before had we experienced such joy at a sporting event. As parents of one of the players, we were ready to celebrate, too. Even the pizza tasted better that night, seasoned with the sweet taste of victory!

> **There were days we wanted to stop this "collision sport" we'd gotten ourselves into.**

But this picture-perfect scene was about to change. After two hours of fun and celebration, it was time to return home. As we drove up to our house, we immediately noticed something was wrong. Bushes were down in the front yard, and piles of some kind of lumpy material were scattered across the yard. Those piles turned out to be mountains of pebbles; it seemed someone had dumped rocks all over our grassy lawn. Worst of all, the vandals had left a nasty note with an even nastier "deposit" on our front doorstep.

After the initial shock of the scene had worn off, we began to realize what had happened. The sore losers had struck our house since Steve been part of the team's coaching staff. We could hardly believe it, until we talked to the team manager about the situation. Apparently, we hadn't been the only target of post-game anger. And anger at what? Anger over a defeat in a Little League championship for ten-year-olds?

As humans, our natural response was to get angry right back. But then we looked at the shocked faces of our two sons, who couldn't believe someone would do this to their home. That's when we realized this was an opportunity for a life lesson for all of us. We knew that we needed to walk through this ugly scenario carefully so we'd set the right example for our children.

It certainly wasn't a life lesson we ever anticipated, and, to be quite honest, it was one that we would rather have avoided our kids witnessing. But this is part of the world in which they live, along with the great, good, and even mundane times they're going to experience. Our job as parents is to help them learn the valuable lessons in these everyday situations. Even the not-so-nice ones.

> *A critical element to these life lessons is finding balance in the teaching and equipping experience.*

So, our children got to watch their parents control their tempers, call the police to take a report, and then spend the next morning cleaning up the mess with as positive an attitude as we could have. We prayed as a family for the culprits, and then we talked through the situation with our sons when we'd had some time to cool down and process more clearly ourselves. Believe us, it wasn't easy, but we knew the real victory from that day would probably come much later because we taught our kids how to handle a good situation gone bad.

Looking for Life Lessons

We didn't have to go looking for that particular life lesson—it found us. And this is true for many of the important day-to-day lessons that we can teach our children. Life happens. Experiences occur each day, throughout all of our waking hours, and sometimes in the sleeping ones, too! As parents, our objective should be three-fold:

1. We have to serve as exceptional role-models through life's many experiences.

2. We must intentionally teach valuable life lessons to children as opportunities arise.
3. We should use life experiences to directly point out the Three Pillars of Faith, Family, and Education.

Whether in our homes, on the road to school, at the shopping mall, during a sporting event, or while doing homework, there are plenty of chances to talk to your kids about how God is using experiences to grow and develop them into the person He hopes they'll become. When they have conflicts with siblings or other family members, these are times to discuss the importance of working things out and making amends so that you'll have a strong, healthy family unit throughout life. School and learning will be a primary part of their developmental years, so you can make these experiences positive for them, encouraging them to strive to do their best because education is a virtue in your family.

> *Be sensitive to each child's developmental stage when processing any life lesson.*

A critical element to these life lessons is finding balance in the teaching and equipping experience. In other words, we don't want to overdo it on the training. If there are too many "here's another life lesson, kids," they'll simply tune out. But if you strategically discuss situations, knowing when to say something about a circumstance and when to just listen, your children will be more likely to "get it" when you do share with them. Part of this balance comes with time and experience, which is why it is helpful to have other good parents as mentors so you can observe and learn from them (we'll discuss more about learning how and when to listen later in the chapter).

The key is being in tune with your kids and being involved in their lives—because that's how you'll find the right opportunities to share with them.

LIFE EXPERIENCE AND YOUR EXCEPTIONAL KIDS

Sometimes the best lessons in life happen by simply being observers of various situations. We remember watching a parent at a fast-food restaurant who was so impatient with the employee (a young teenager, more than likely in his first job). The mother of three started getting upset with the worker, and then she raised her voice so she could let everyone around her know how incompetent she thought his service was. The young employee turned red from embarrassment, and so did this lady's children. Our boys looked at us in surprise at her actions, and we were reminded about how much our kids learn by watching people around them. Needless to say, we had a good conversation later about how inappropriate that woman's actions were!

As we mentioned in Chapter 4 on Self-Discipline, circumstances will naturally arise day-in and day-out where kids will make decisions, some great and others not-so-great. These too become excellent opportunities for conversations that extend well beyond the momentary situation. Have a talk right then and there about why the choice they made was a good one and how that will benefit them now and later. Perhaps you can share an example from your own life that will reinforce the lesson, and help them understand you are still in the learning and growing process, too.

> *It's our opinion that your kids don't need to know every intimate detail about you. In fact, they are on a "need to know" basis!*

Let them think through and discuss bad decisions they've made before you discuss consequences. Even young children can be asked something like, "Haley, why was taking your brother's candy from him not a kind thing to do? Would you want that to happen to you?" Let older kids consider the long-term consequences of bad choices, like what might happen if they were eighteen and they took something that didn't belong to them. Ask teenagers and young adults about their feelings since they're more in touch with emotions during these years of development.

Remember, be sensitive to each child's developmental stage when processing any life lesson. For instance, younger children who are in the "concrete" stage of life will need simple, straightforward examples and discussions, while older kids who think more "abstractly" will be able to consider and discuss deeper issues and the bigger picture.

> **Believe us, your children know you aren't perfect.**

Here are some other thoughts about what might stimulate life lesson discussions:

- Personal family struggles
- Problems their friends are experiencing
- Local, national, or global news items
- Church or community issues
- School-related concerns
- Extra-curricular activities
- Their own *interpersonal* circumstances and *intrapersonal* thoughts and feelings

As we mentioned above, sometimes our own experiences are important to share with kids as they grow and develop, in part because we should strive to help our children avoid some of the painful and problematic mistakes we made along life's journey. In fact, this is exactly what Moses reminded the children of Israel they were to do after their tumultuous experiences in Egypt:

"Remember today that your children were not the ones who saw and experienced the discipline of the LORD your God: his majesty, his mighty hand, his outstretched arm; the signs he performed and the things he did in the heart of Egypt, both to Pharaoh king of Egypt and to his whole country; what he did to

the Egyptian army, to its horses and chariots, how he overwhelmed them with the waters of the Red Sea as they were pursuing you, and how the LORD brought lasting ruin on them. It was not your children who saw what he did for you in the wilderness until you arrived at this place"* (Deuteronomy 11:2–5).

The parents of these children, however, *had* been the ones who had seen and witnessed numerous miracles and interventions by the Lord. Were they to bottle them up, keep them as "family secrets," and then carry them to their graves? No! The rest of God's directives to the adults included the following:

"Fix these words of mine in your hearts and minds; tie them as symbols on your hands and bind them on your foreheads. Teach them to your children, talking about them when you sit at home and when you walk along the road, when you lie down and when you get up. Write them on the doorframes of your houses and on your gates" (Deuteronomy 11:18–20).

> *Moms and dads must find the right balance between protecting their kids from "life" and letting them venture into the real-world so they can learn from those experiences.*

Just as He did in Deuteronomy 6, God reminded parents that children need to be taught the historical lessons as well as His virtues and commandments. When individuals understand why guidelines are important and for their own good, they are much more likely to want to follow them!

And God gives a promise to people who choose to follow His Straight Lines for living. Remember this return on the investment? *"So that your days and the days of your children may be many in the land the LORD*

> *Balance is what parents should strive for so they can keep their children well-balanced in life, too.*

> *Yet, as your sons and daughters grow and develop, so must their life experiences.*

swore to give your ancestors, as many as the days that the heavens are above the earth" (Deuteronomy 11:21).

Now parents, does this mean you need to share every detail of your past life or previous sins? Of course not! We've had some moms and dads ask us if they should talk about promiscuity when they were teenagers or experimentation with drugs in college. It's our opinion that your kids don't need to know every intimate detail about you. In fact, they are on a "need to know" basis! But you can share in generalities, especially with older teenagers and young adults if you feel the life lesson would be more meaningful with such openness.

Some parents ask us, "Isn't this being deceitful? Shouldn't our kids know we are sinners?" Believe us, your children know you aren't perfect—ours certainly found out early enough! They didn't need to have all of the details of our past that we'd already been forgiven by God for. Instead, what our kids need to understand is that their parents are still learning, too, and when we make mistakes, we take ownership for them and we make things right immediately.

Just as those followers of old were to instruct their children about what they'd learned from the Lord, so should we. Exceptional children who are going to become inspirational adults must receive this kind of regular, consistent instruction from their parents who are actively looking for opportunities to make connections through real-life experiences.

THE OVER-PROTECTIVE VERSUS UNDER-FUNCTIONING PARENT

The parenting process can sometimes seem overwhelming for mothers and fathers. Even perusing bookstore shelves and online listings for material on parenting is a daunting task. Plus, some of us struggle with our own history of the parenting experience, trying to take what was good from those developmental days and address shortcomings from previous generations so we can change and make things better for our kids.

This was our experience as parents, too, and it's a big reason we chose to hone what we had learned, read about, and experienced in our personal and professional lives into these Straight Line Strategies. This section in particular focuses on a critical lesson for parents who want to raise exceptional children: moms and dads must find the right balance between protecting their kids from "life" and letting them venture into the real-world so they can learn from those experiences.

In other words, some parents can be over-protective while others are under-functioning. These are two opposing ends of the parenting process, and focusing at either end of the spectrum will not empower kids to become exceptional. Balance is what parents should strive for so they can keep their children well-balanced in life, too.

> *We must use a similar inoculation process when it comes to other not-so-nice aspects of living in an imperfect environment.*

Now, let us start by sharing what we are *not* saying. We are *not* saying that you shouldn't protect your children, and we are *not* suggesting that you can't let your kids go through some experiences on their own. Actually, great parents will have to walk the balance beam of this life lesson throughout their children's developmental years. Some days it will be much easier than others (as we've said earlier, it's far easier to protect them when they're in a playpen). Yet, as your sons and daughters grow and develop, so must their life experiences.

For example, both of our boys wanted to play sports, which we encouraged since this seemed to be an area of interest for both of them. The initial years were easy, because Pee Wee sports were all about positive reinforcement and praise. Everyone got to play, and every child got a ribbon or trophy at the end of the season.

But then the day finally arrived when our oldest wanted to play Pop Warner football. We knew what this meant from watching the bigger kids on the practice fields. The degree of competition was more intense, and so were the coaches. Our son would probably be yelled at like the other boys were when they lagged behind or didn't run a play correctly. Yes, our precious, wonderful boy might even have to run extra laps if he didn't measure up to these coaches' expectations!

> *Parents who want to bring up exceptional kids look for real-time and real-life opportunities to point out critical life lessons that must be learned before adulthood.*

Did we keep our kids out of these experiences because we wanted to protect them? No way! We knew if they wanted to play at this level, they'd have to experience some "real world" stuff in the process. But we didn't let them simply go out there and get hammered, either. We sat them down and explained that their coaches would be tough, and they might even hear language that we didn't condone. We set up the proper expectations for what they might experience, and then let them know they could talk to us any time about concerns they might have along the way.

> *This balance requires you to "become an expert in your child—"*

And we kept that dialogue going, making sure they were doing okay with every activity in which they were involved.

Did we cringe when our boys were yelled at? Sure—especially Rebecca, who sometimes wanted to take her "baby" home and keep him safe! But we firmly believe that *not* letting our children see and experience real life would have harmed them even further, because one day in the not-so-distant future, they were going to have these kind of experiences anyway, and we wanted them to be equipped for those situations.

We have always felt that it was far better to help our children through real-life experiences while we were there to guide them, talk with them, and, yes, even cry through some of life's ups and downs with them than to entirely avoid issues that they'd eventually have to face. We call this "The Inoculation Principle." The Inoculation Principle in parenting is much like that of inoculations for diseases. We give our babies, toddlers, and children little doses of something that's not so good for them (like measles, mumps, chicken pox) so they'll be *immune* from that illness for the rest of their lives. We must use a similar inoculation process when it comes to other not-so-nice aspects of living in an imperfect environment.

> *Good listening is somewhat of a lost art form in our busy, bustling, and noise-bombarded society.*

Parents, the world that your kids live in isn't like Disneyland. Yes, it can be wonderful. Sometimes it's a bit wacky. And, sadly, it is also desperately wicked. To overly-protect your kids during their developmental years from these realities is doing them a grave disservice. On the other hand, to simply put your kids into situations with little or no guidance is at best ignorance and, at worst, parental negligence.

Exceptional parents must determine what the healthy balance of real-life experience will look like for each of their children. They must "inoculate" their kids with small doses of those bad, negative, and sinful aspects of life that their kids need to learn about, while at the same time protecting them from any kind of overdose!

Parents who want to bring up exceptional kids look for real-time and real-life opportunities to point out critical life lessons that must be learned before adulthood. Mothers and fathers must stay involved in each of their children's lives so they know who their friends are, what they're watching on television, what music they're downloading, and what they're doing in their free time. They must be involved in a very hands-on way when kids are younger, and always communicatively as they grow older.

This balance requires you to "become an expert in your child—" the philosophy we've been sharing with you. Remember Proverbs 22:6? You are to train up your son or daughter in the "way he [or she] should go," which literally means according to his or her way. Each of your children will have different likes, dislikes, abilities, hopes and dreams. Likewise, they will also respond to their world in distinctly unique ways. Some kids will be much more sensitive and thus need more protection from certain elements in life. Others will be quite adventurous and therefore will need you to "pull in the reins" when they want to go too far.

> *Hearing isn't our problem—listening is. Listening involves total focus on the individual who is sharing.*

Exceptional parents who want to raise motivated, curious, caring, competent children will let them experience real-life as is age-appropriate and with regular, consistent guidance. These moms and dads realize that the years they have to teach lessons through these life experiences are precious and fleeting, so they'll use each and every day to assist their children in learning how to navigate the sometimes confusing by-ways and highways of the world.

LEARNING TO BE GREAT LISTENERS

Many of the best "teachable moments" we have experienced as parents have come when we were practicing the art of good listening. Sometimes this happened when our kids started sharing about their lives over cereal at the breakfast table. On other occasions, we might be driving along in the car and a conversation came up unexpectedly because of something our boys were processing. Many memorable moments came at bedtime, when we just sat with our boys and listened to the final thoughts on their minds before they drifted off to sleep.

> *Listening means an intentional effort to process, understand, and do something with the information you are receiving.*

Good listening is somewhat of a lost art form in our busy, bustling, and noise-bombarded society. Everywhere we go people are talking, music is playing, and cell phones are pinging or ringing. Hearing isn't our problem—listening is.

Listening involves total focus on the individual who is sharing. It means not only are our mouths closed (except perhaps when we need to ask a clarifying question) as the other person speaks, but it also means our minds are tuned off to the other things in our lives and tuned-in to the one with whom we are interacting. So if your child is prattling on about something, but you are thinking about work or making dinner, you may be hearing what he or she is saying, but you definitely aren't listening.

We love the Parable of the Sower that's found in Matthew 13 because of what Jesus had to say about listening. When the disciples asked the Lord why He often spoke in parables, he quoted a section of Scripture found in Isaiah:

"You will be ever hearing but never understanding; you will be ever seeing but never perceiving. For this people's heart has become calloused; they hardly

> *"You have two ears and one mouth for a reason" is so poignant. We should be listening at least twice as much as we are talking!*

hear with their ears, and they have closed their eyes. Otherwise they might see with their eyes, hear with their ears, understand with their hearts and turn, and I would heal them" (Matthew 13:14–15).

> *"Teachable moments" will require a moment of insight, a word of encouragement, a simple reminder about a life lesson, or even a Scripture that ties into what they've just talked about.*

The Lord explained to His disciples that lots of people would hear what He shared about Heaven and God's plan for them, but just like today, not everyone would truly listen. Listening means an intentional effort to process, understand, and do something with the information you are receiving. When applied to our topic, this means that we should be parents who both listen and understand!

Many times after He shared a story, Jesus would say, *"whoever has ears, let them hear"* (13:9). Who has ears? Virtually everyone on the planet! So the act of listening shouldn't be as hard as it is if we choose to really focus on the message. That's why the expression "you have two ears and one mouth for a reason" is so poignant. We should be listening at least twice as much as we are talking!

Parents, this lesson on listening is critical for two reasons:

1. When we truly listen to our children, we're going to understand who they are as individuals, how they process information, what's important to them, and what they need from us in terms of counsel and guidance.
2. When we actively role-model good listening skills, our kids will pick up those abilities, too. They will see and hear what it means to be active listeners!

In fact, the Lord followed up His thoughts on listening this way: *"But blessed are your eyes because they see, and your ears because they hear" (Matthew 13:16).* Those who will listen will be blessed. As a parent, you'll be blessed by really being able to connect with your kids, and then doubly blessed by raising your children to become exceptional listeners.

So, when should parents listen rather than talk?

1. When kids are sharing a story or scenario that's important to them.
2. When children or teenagers are emotional about an issue and simply need to pour their hearts out.
3. When someone is angry—whether it is the kids or parents. Give everyone time to cool down before a deeper conversation ensues.
4. When your kids specifically say, "I just want to share something with you; I don't need an answer"—or something like this.

> *We wanted our children to experience the "real world" while we still had an opportunity to walk through those experiences with them.*

All of these scenarios should be a signal for you to step back, take a deep breath, and simply listen to your children. When they are finished speaking, you may want to add something like, "Thanks for sharing—I appreciate your clear communication. How about if we table this topic and revisit it later?"

During other conversations, your kids need and may even ask for your input. Remember, you should listen as they share—and part of that conversation may involve you asking clarifying questions like, "So when you told me about that problem at school, did you mean that—?" or "I didn't quite understand what you meant when you told me about—. Could you explain that to me one more time?"

Good listeners also make great eye contact and respond with visual cues and body language that reveal interest, empathy, and understanding. Then, when it's appropriate, the listeners should give feedback. To be honest, sometimes your kids will just want to vent or share and don't want any information from you at all, just like when you come home from a bad day and simply need to get things off your chest. The last thing you want is for someone to give you a lecture or "mini-lesson" during those moments! The same is true for your kids.

> *Princes and princesses must grow up, so we want them to become kings and queens who will mightily impact the kingdom of God!*

But there will be many instances when these "teachable moments" will require a moment of insight, a word of encouragement, a simple reminder about a life lesson, or even a Scripture that ties into what they've just talked about. Again, this can be a bit of a balancing act for parents—trying to figure out when to talk and when to listen. Yet by discovering this balance, you will be able to equip your children with even more real-life lessons than you could ever imagine!

THE MAKING OF A KING AND QUEEN

Several years ago, we had some parents ask us why we would ever allow our children to experience negative life circumstances. They were particularly interested in why we had chosen to put our boys in a large public high school instead of sending them to the excellent Christian school nearby.

Our answer was simple: we wanted our children to experience the "real world" while we still had an opportunity to walk through those experiences with them. Both of us had attended a wonderful private high school—but believe us, this was not a totally protective environment. Why? Because life happens! Real-world stuff is everywhere, even at private and parochial schools! To ignore this reality and hope that bad things or negative influences won't touch our kids is a tragic mistake.

Of course, our natural instinct as exceptional parents is to protect our little princes and princesses! And why not? They are precious creations made in the image of God. Great parents are called to protect, provide for, and pray for their children. However, we are also to "breed 'em up" so they can become inspirational adults who will do awesome things for the Lord all of the days of their lives.

Princes and princesses must grow up, so we want them to become kings and queens who will mightily impact the kingdom of God!

When we review the lives of David and Esther, there's no real indication of just how exceptional they'd become. David was a shepherd boy, one of many children in an ordinary Jewish family. Esther was an orphan being raised by her cousin in a foreign land among people who weren't exactly fond of her Jewish heritage.

> *Their Heavenly Father had a destiny for each of them that probably far exceeded their parents' hopes and dreams.*

Notice that both David and Esther weren't insulated from real life. In fact, as a shepherd, David had to be out with the flocks and protect them from dangerous predators (see I Samuel 17 regarding his fight with a lion and a bear). Esther's parents had died, so her cousin Mordecai became her guardian after she was orphaned (Esther 2). Yet both of these exceptional young people would go on to positions of authority and power, greatly influencing their people and history for generations to come.

> *As exceptional parents, we get to serve as our children's guides in the specific time God has placed them in, teaching them the lessons of Faith, Family, and Education so they can positively impact their world.*

Despite how David and Esther's parents might have wanted to protect them, real life happened, and their

Heavenly Father had a destiny for each of them that probably far exceeded their parents' hopes and dreams. Despite living in an imperfect world, these exceptional kids would leave a lasting legacy because of their strong foundation of faith in God (we'll delve more deeply into the importance of legacy in Chapter 9).

We might conclude that David and Esther's real-life experiences were exactly what was needed to prepare them for the challenges they would face in their respective futures. If they had been totally insulated from their community and culture, they might not have been as savvy when their enemies came after them, or when less-than-perfect circumstances arose (for instance, when David faced Goliath, and when Haman tried to destroy Esther's people).

> *Our little princes and princesses will acquire the skill sets necessary to rule their world one day.*

These stories from Scripture don't mean that we have to take our sons into the wilderness to face wild animals like David or put our daughters into beauty pageants like Esther, yet we certainly must provide them with learning experiences from the world in which they live in order to properly prepare them to face its challenges. As exceptional parents, we get to serve as our children's guides in the specific time God has placed them in, teaching them the lessons of Faith, Family, and Education so they can positively impact their world. By actively providing opportunities for our children to learn through daily experiences, our little princes and princesses will acquire the skill sets necessary to rule their world one day.

So, look for opportunities to teach your children from their earliest days. Use everyday experiences as teaching tools for crucial Straight Line lessons. Practice the art of good listening, but then speak up when the time is right in order to share insights that are vital for your kids' development into exceptional human beings. This kind of parenting will never be boring, and you'll be leaving behind the greatest legacy you could ever hope to achieve.

My Straight Line NAV System

Birth–5: During these early developmental years, give your children many opportunities to experience their world alongside you. Take your babies on long walks, let them interact with others, and talk to them about what they are seeing, hearing, tasting, smelling, and feeling. Share God's amazing world with them, and watch them begin to blossom!

6–12: As children move through the concrete/developmental to the abstract thinking years, be sure to adjust your teaching and conversations accordingly. Get your kids involved in various activities that pique their interest, and keep in touch with what they're learning and who their friends are. Practice active listening, and then look for the right moments to share life lessons with them.

13–20+: Teenagers and young adults begin experiencing more and more of the adult world, especially in the technological age we live in. Keep conversations going by showing you are interested in their lives. When they are ready to talk, listen! Most of all, look for those "teachable moments" when they'll be apt to hear what you've got to say!

Chapter 9

Leaving a Lasting Legacy

Strategy #9: Exceptional parents intentionally encourage their children to pass the Straight Lines for being exceptional to the next generation.

Nestled in the wooded hills of Tennessee, an antebellum home became the setting for our oldest son's wedding. There are so many things in life you can't really prepare for, and this lovely occasion was one of them. As Ryan and Lindsey walked down the aisle, our hearts filled with love, joy, and a myriad of other indescribable emotions.

We couldn't help but reflect on the road that had led us to this special celebration. That journey had also been filled with love, joy, emotional moments, and lots and lots of hard work! We'd actually been praying for our son's wife since before either one of them was born, and there she stood, much more amazing than any creation we could have designed ourselves.

We also felt a tremendous amount of peace while we listened to the pastor perform the ceremony because we had great confidence that all of our efforts wouldn't end once their vows were exchanged. Instead, we knew our son and his wife would keep living out those Straight Line Strategies and intentionally pass them to the next generation.

Several years have passed since their wedding, and we have observed many confirmations of those thoughts and feelings. Our children continue to live a life of faith—one that they have made their own. Even though their lives are quite busy, they are still extremely invested in family. And our kids are committed to education, as we've witnessed their continued growth, both personally and professionally. We're proud of them, but we are also proud of the legacy we're leaving behind through them!

DEFINING LEGACY

The topic of legacy has been in vogue in the business world for a number of years, partially fueled by Baby Boomers who aspire to leave their mark on society. But legacy is a very old concept. In fact, it comes from the Latin terms "legatum" or "lego," which mean to ordain, appoint, or bequeath. In other words, something important would be left behind for someone else to benefit from and build upon.

> *Our children continue to live a life of faith—one that they have made their own.*

Parents, this is exactly what these Straight Line Strategies are meant to do. Your most important legacy will be your children. What will they be like? How will they live? What good things have you imparted over the course of their lifetime that will be passed on to future generations in your family?

Sadly, many people today don't even consider the topic of legacy until they are nearing retirement, or even the end of life itself. That's way too late! Legacy must start right here, right now. Your legacy—and your children's legacy—begins with this new day and how you choose to live it.

> *Your most important legacy will be your children.*

We watched a television show recently where some aging rock stars were asked what they thought their legacy would be. They stumbled and bumbled for a bit, then came up with a few phrases like "We partied hard," and "We totally rocked our world." *Really?* This is what they hoped to be remembered for? And, tragically, not one of them mentioned anything about family or their children and future generations!

In our world today, legacy often boils down to monetary and tangible aspects of what we've accomplished. For instance, some people want to leave behind large amounts of money for their kids and grandkids so they'll

> *Sadly, many people today don't even consider the topic of legacy until they are nearing retirement, or even the end of life itself.*

"be secure." While this is a nice gesture, money can't be all that we consider when we think about the future. Money can be spent, wasted, and even disappear due to fraud, but the lessons on how to live a satisfying life transcend time.

Actually, these Straight Line Strategies not only transcend time, but they also hold their value for millennia! They were true in the Iron Age, and they're still true in the Space Age. These truths are based on God's guidelines and principles, and, as we like to say, why mess with the Creator's design for great living?

So this discussion begs a critical question: *what kind of legacy are you creating?* Are you more focused on saving for your kids' college someday than teaching them the skill sets they need to become motivated, curious, caring, competent individuals who will exceed expectations? Are you strategizing over long-term financial investments—or are you contemplating the lasting benefits of investing time in the Straight Line approaches you've been reading about?

There are a few main goals for exceptional parents who want to leave an exceptional legacy:

1. You must raise your children to live to their highest potential, exceed expectations, and become inspirational adults one day.
2. You must regularly and consistently reinforce that your kids don't have to *be* the best, but they must *do* their best!
3. You must focus on your children replicating these Straight Line Strategies in their lives and in the lives of others, including the next generation.
4. You must be *actively* and *intentionally* engaged in the parenting process all throughout life's journey.

Parents, we can't be asleep at the wheel and expect great results in our kids one day! We cannot expect others to teach these skill sets for us, and we certainly shouldn't expect our children to "pick up" the essential pillars of Faith, Family, and Education on their own! Just like all roads in life, there are specific lines to follow that will get us to the end of our journey safely and successfully.

> **The lessons on how to live a satisfying life transcend time.**

Consider life like any other trip you'd take. Do you ever start an important journey without knowing where you want to end up? Of course not! That's why exceptional parents must envision *exactly* where we want our children to be—one, five, ten, twenty, even thirty years from now! We've also got to follow the specific Straight Lines that will get us to that final destination. Then, and only then, will our children be able to carry on the journey smoothly, because they'll have the right guidelines to follow, which we've carefully been developing in them over time.

> **You must raise your children to live to their highest potential.**

Exceptional parents begin thinking about legacy—theirs as well as their children's—early and often. The next step involves actually talking to your children about the concept of legacy. They need to understand that what they do today matters tomorrow, and people do indeed reap what's been sown. Exceptional parents help their children realize the importance of making good choices and upholding their family's standards. Teaching our kids about legacy will always include the proverb that states: "A good name is more desirable than great riches; to be esteemed is better than silver or gold" (Proverbs 22:1).

> *You must regularly and consistently reinforce that your kids don't have to be the best, but they must do their best!*

Individuals who are striving only to leave behind money or material things for the next generation need to know that won't buy a good name. This is a legacy that is earned over time, and that's what great parents want for their exceptional children. Your utmost desire should be to minimize circumstances that would take away from their success while maximizing every opportunity to impart God's guidelines and Straight Line Strategies that lead to exceptional living!

NO MONEY-BACK GUARANTEE

While we are living in an increasingly entitled society where some people think they deserve things simply because of their mere existence, we need to look carefully at this kind of attitude's impact on all of us. We may disapprove of individuals who view the world from a "you owe me" perspective, yet if we are quite honest, as parents, we can often feel entitled, too, especially when it comes to raising kids.

> *You must focus on your children replicating these Straight Line Strategies.*

What do we mean? Well, after years of work and effort, many parents feel like they "deserve" to have great kids. And for those who really have put in lots of time and energy, following as many of the Straight Line Strategies and godly principles as possible, they often believe that God *should* bless them with exceptional children—no exceptions.

The problem is, there are exceptions. Over the years, we've watched incredible families end up with a wild child, and the parents aren't quite sure what to do in order to get their boy or girl back on track. Some amazing families also raise good, but average kids, with no real signs of being "exceptional." Then there are the families that really skew the data. These parents don't seem to do much of anything, yet their children outshine their peers in academics, athletics, community service, communication skills, and interpersonal relationships.

> *Parents, we can't be asleep at the wheel and expect great results in our kids one day!*

At this juncture in our journey, we must share this reality with you: *when you follow all the Straight Line Strategies we've given and strive to have God guide you and your family, you may not get the motivated, curious, caring competent children you hoped for and dreamed about.*

How is that possible? Because while exceptions exist in raising kids, guarantees don't. In a fallen world, humans falter and fail. With free choice and the reality of sin in life, our children can make great decisions, or very, very bad ones.

> *Just like all roads in life, there are specific lines to follow that will get us to the end of our journey safely and successfully.*

However, we can also tell you after years of experience and work with parents who have implemented these Straight Lines regularly and consistently, the chances are *much* greater that you and your children will experience success now and in the future! Basically, you can minimize mediocrity and maximize your kids' chances of being exceptional.

In fact, we have never received a single call from parents who were dissatisfied after applying these principles. Instead, many have assured us that these Straight Line Strategies greatly assisted them in the parenting process. These moms and dads usually report that their children, while not perfect, are moving along a path that is healthy, well-balanced, and even inspiring!

> *Exceptional parents begin thinking about legacy—theirs as well as their children's—early and often.*

This is a huge piece in the legacy puzzle. While there are no money-back guarantees in parenting, we're confident these guidelines increase opportunities for success. How can we be so certain? After thirty years of professional and personal experiences, we've seen these Straight Line Strategies pay off for hundreds of families. And while you may be uncertain about how your kids are going to turn out, eventually they should "get" the principles you are imparting to them, even though, for some, it might be years down the road.

The parents who fail to pass on these Straight Lines tend to have an equal, but opposite result. Their children, who didn't receive specific guidelines or godly principles for successful living, often struggle—sometimes for years or over their entire lifetime. Even if the parents are dedicated and exceptional people, their success will end with them if they don't pass on what they've

> *Your utmost desire should be to minimize circumstances that would take away from their success while maximizing every opportunity to impart God's guidelines and Straight Line Strategies that lead to exceptional living!*

learned to their children. An example of this tragedy is found in Judges 2.

"After Joshua had dismissed the Israelites, they went to take possession of the land, each to their own inheritance. The people served the LORD throughout the lifetime of Joshua and of the elders who outlived him and who had seen all the great things the LORD had done for Israel. Joshua son of Nun, the servant of the LORD, died at the age of a hundred and ten. And they buried him in the land of his inheritance" (2:6–9a).

> *If we are quite honest, as parents, we can often feel entitled, too, especially when it comes to raising kids.*

Joshua was the man who took Moses' place, leading the children of Israel when he died. Joshua was a strong, faithful leader, one who obviously passed on God's principles to the people because they we're reported to have "served the Lord" during his lifetime and the lifetime of those elders he had trained to carry on his legacy. Sounds great so far, right? Well, let's keep reading:

> *With free choice and the reality of sin in life, our children can make great decisions, or very, very bad ones.*

"After that whole generation had been gathered to their ancestors, another generation grew up who knew neither the LORD nor what he had done for Israel. Then the Israelites did evil in the eyes of the LORD" (Joshua 2:10–11).

Something went desperately wrong with the generation of men, women, and children who followed Joshua and his elders. Once these senior members of society had died, the next generation didn't even know the Lord! These verses reveal that they didn't have a basic knowledge of all that God had done for their parents and grandparents while in Egypt and during their fight for freedom in this new land. They were ignorant of their amazing legacy, and they actually lived lives in direct opposition to God's principles.

What had happened in just one generation? While the Bible doesn't spell it out, we can make some pretty good assumptions:

1. The parents didn't teach their children the history of how God had worked in their lives.
2. The parents failed to instill godly principles for living in their children, not even the basics of faith in the Lord.
3. The parents appeared to have not even lived a visibly holy life, full of Straight Lines, so that their kids would strive to follow their godly example.

> *You can minimize mediocrity and maximize your kids' chances of being exceptional.*

This is the epitome of parental negligence! What exactly *were* they doing? What were those parents talking about at home, on the road, before they went to bed, and when they woke up? Did they ever once consider the legacy they'd leave behind—in this case, a generation of degenerates who "*aroused the LORD's anger because they forsook him and served Baal and the Ashtoreths. In his anger against Israel the LORD gave them into the hands of raiders who plundered them. He sold them into the hands of their enemies all around, whom they were no longer able to resist. Whenever Israel went out to fight, the hand of the LORD was against them to defeat them, just as he had sworn to them. They were in great distress*" (Judges 2:12b–15).

> *While there are no money-back guarantees in parenting, we're confident these guidelines increase opportunities for success.*

How tragic! This generation, without guidelines and godless, suffered the consequences of not having received an intentional legacy of faith. Their enemies surrounded them, and they succumbed to their control. The consequences for selling out to sin instead of embracing the Lord's Straight Lines eventually caused them great distress.

> *The consequences for selling out to sin instead of embracing the Lord's Straight Lines eventually caused them great distress.*

Parents, if this isn't a call to prepare for battle on behalf of your children, we don't know what is! Your family can turn from totally on fire for God to testing out the flames of hell itself in one short generation. And the only ones to stop this generational freefall are you and the Lord. By following His directives, teaching His principles, and intentionally talking to your kids about a godly legacy, the probability for success in the next generation is not only good—it's great!

Sure, nothing in life is guaranteed, especially when it comes to parenting, but by doing the right things (parents first, then our children), the chances for an exceptional outcome are exponentially better. And guess what? You've got plenty of work ahead of you! This effort in legacy continues all the way until you're ready for Heaven!

THE NOT-SO-EMPTY NEST

The previous generation talked a lot about the empty nest—how to adjust, what to do with the time they previously spent on parenting, etc. We're here to tell you that the current generation of parents is discussing something completely different: *we don't want an empty nest, and we never intend to have one!*

Many twenty-first century parents realize their God-given role isn't to mourn the loss of children but to continue to develop the "next best nest" that we possibly can. This means that parents are still needed by their children and, eventually, grandchildren. The job of exceptional parenting isn't finished when the kids go to college; instead, it's morphing and transitioning.

The stark difference between the attitude of some in the previous generation and that of today's parents can be summed up in an email we received not long ago. A forty-something mother of teenagers wrote us because she was beginning to worry about the "empty nest" syndrome others told her was coming. Part of her dilemma was that she and her husband held very different feelings than their parents had about their kids approaching adulthood. She summed up their thoughts this way:

"I am not sure what to do with myself. I think this is a new challenge for our generation and not something our parents dealt with—they couldn't wait for us to leave!"

> *Your family can turn from totally on fire for God to testing out the flames of hell itself in one short generation.*

What a sad sentiment for someone to verbalize, but, believe us, she isn't alone. From our counseling clinic to our leadership consulting, many mothers and fathers have shared that they wonder why the older generation couldn't wait to launch them into the world. Twenty-first century "helicopter parents," as they've been labeled by society, can't understand that kind of thinking. Instead, they long for a continuing relationship with their offspring that will last a lifetime. They want to spend *more* time with their kids as they age, and they hope their children will feel the same way, too!

This philosophy is part of exceptional parenting: moms and dads are called to their roles as parents all of the days of their lives!

An interesting story is tucked away in Isaiah 38. It reveals the tale of good King Hezekiah, who had fallen gravely ill and was told by the prophet who wrote this book of his eminent demise. Instead of accepting the death sentence, Hezekiah went directly to God in prayer. Because of his faith, the Lord granted him extra time (fifteen more years, to be exact), and in his prayer of thanksgiving, Hezekiah proclaimed these words:

"For the grave cannot praise you, death cannot sing your praise; those who go down to the pit cannot hope for your faithfulness. The living, the living—they praise you, as I am doing today; parents tell their children about your faithfulness" (Isaiah 38:18–19).

In his near-death experience, this godly king recognized many significant facts, including that it was the parents' job to tell children about God's faithfulness. They were responsible for singing His praises, and, by doing so, they let the next generation know just how great the Lord truly is!

> *By following His directives, teaching His principles, and intentionally talking to your kids about a godly legacy, the probability for success in the next generation is not only good—it's great!*

Parents, when do you think that role of passing on God's truths and praising Him ends? When your kids turn eighteen? When they graduate from college? When they move out on their own? *No way!* Imparting Straight Line Strategies and principles about the Lord's love, goodness, and grace don't end at a certain age. There's no retiring from the parenting process, and that's fabulous news for anyone who fears the empty nest syndrome! Now, this doesn't mean you will parent the same way you did when your kids were in elementary school or high school. You will need to transition your parenting skill sets along with them as they transition into adulthood.

What we're suggesting to you, though, is that there really should never be an empty nest. Instead, parents of teenagers and young adults should be putting the finishing touches on the "next-best nest." Our *physical* nest will change, but nurturing and spiritual development are merely transforming. While our fledgling young adults are learning to fly, we get to stick nearby to make sure they survive the first flight (or second or third) into the world of independence. Like the eagle, we don't just hurl them out into the world and fly off on vacation. No, we hover close by (good news for helicopter parents) until we're certain they can make it on their own.

> *Moms and dads are called to their roles as parents all of the days of their lives!*

This isn't time for us to retire to Bermuda either! Our kids still need guidance. After all, did the Lord let us go completely on our own when we got saved? Of course not! In fact, He sent His Holy Spirit to be with us—guiding, instructing, and yes, even comforting us, whenever we need assurance. Our Heavenly Father doesn't leave us to figure life out on our own, so why do earthly parents think they should totally abandon ship just because they've been on the job a few decades?

Parents, this is a huge part of your ongoing legacy. Working diligently at passing on these Straight Lines will be your long-term investment in the future, but you still must manage your investment all the way until your eternal retirement. Even adult kids desperately need your wisdom and advice. They require you to be actively involved in their lives.

> *When do you think that role of passing on God's truths and praising Him ends?*

You won't be as "hands-on" as when they were three or thirteen, but twenty-three, thirty-three, and forty-three-year-olds still need parents! Plus, they will watch as you keep growing and developing, so they'll follow your Straight Lines throughout adulthood, too!

Do you get to have fun in this next, best season of life? You bet you do! As we stated before, we're thoroughly enjoying watching our sons—now young men—make principled decisions on their own. We are experiencing so much joy seeing them transition into their careers, marry amazing young women, and move on to the next phases in their lives. And soon, very soon, we are well aware that our nest will be filling up again with the next generation in the legacy we're leaving.

> *There's no retiring from the parenting process, and that's fabulous news for anyone who fears the empty nest syndrome!*

Sure, there are some days when we're a bit melancholy because we miss the days of "Mommy, Daddy, I need you!" or tucking them in at night, saying a prayer, and sending them off to sleep with a song. But God didn't design kids to stay kids forever. His plan is for them to become the most motivated, curious, caring, competent, and inspirational adults you could ever possibly imagine. So keep helping them get there!

WELCOME TO THE HALL OF FAME

The concept of vision—envisioning what your legacy will look like when it's time to leave this life and move into the next—is critical to the entire legacy process. Will you look back over the years and be filled with regret and shame, or will you be ready to celebrate your membership in the "Parenting Hall of Fame?"

> *Our Heavenly Father doesn't leave us to figure life out on our own, so why do earthly parents think they should totally abandon ship just because they've been on the job a few decades?*

Believe it or not, this is one Hall of Fame any parent can strive for! Your children, their children, and all of those who follow after will remember the way you lived better than any other single item you might bequeath them. Your kids will tell stories about you for years on end. What do you want those tales to include? Can you picture the fond memories your kids, grandkids, and great-grandkids will treasure?

Take a few minutes and ask yourself, what do you want your children to be like as adults? Will they be motivated, curious, caring, competent men and women who exceed expectations? Will they inspire others in their sphere of influence, especially in terms of the Three Pillars of Faith, Family, and Education? Will they pass on the skills sets for Self-Discipline, Personal Responsibility, and Relational Equity to their own children and grandchildren?

Spend some time now envisioning exactly what you'd like your family to look like in the future. Next, you must follow those Straight Line Strategies that are going to take you from where you are to where you want to be. Getting started, you may feel like you're taking baby steps, but keep going. Keep growing! Your consistent effort is the only way your children will ever have a chance to become the exceptional individuals God desires them to become.

> *Working diligently at passing on these Straight Lines will be your long-term investment in the future, but you still must manage your investment all the way until your eternal retirement.*

We never know how much time we have in this all-important parenting process to get Hall of Fame status. Let's take a look at some incredible young people from ages past that remind us of this important fact:

"*Then the king ordered Ashpenaz, chief of his court officials, to bring into the king's service some of the Israelites from the royal family and the nobility— young men without any physical defect, handsome, showing aptitude for every kind of learning, well informed, quick to understand, and qualified to serve in the* king's palace. He was to teach them the language and literature of the Babylonians. The king assigned them a daily amount of food and wine from the king's table. They were to be trained for three years, and after that they were to enter the king's service. Among those who were chosen were some from Judah: Daniel, Hananiah, Mishael and Azariah. The chief official gave them new names: to Daniel, the name Belteshazzar; to Hananiah, Shadrach; to Mishael, Meshach; and to Azariah, Abednego" (Daniel 1:3–7).

> You won't be as "hands-on" as when they were three or thirteen, but twenty-three, thirty-three, and forty-three-year-olds still need parents!

Daniel, Shadrach, Meshach, and Abednego are four famous characters from the Bible, but we have absolutely no idea who their parents were. However, we believe they ought to be included in the Parenting Hall of Fame. We don't feel this way because they had certain position or power or prestige (which they probably did since the king only took young men who came from the families of royalty and nobility). Rather, they seem to have been exceptional parents because whatever Straight Lines they taught and equipping they practiced with their children took hold early! In fact, the godly principles they seem to have imparted to their children allowed these young men to behave exceptionally when it mattered most.

> God didn't design kids to stay kids forever. His plan is for them to become the most motivated, curious, caring, competent, and inspirational adults you could ever possibly imagine. So keep helping them get there!

These four men were taken into the king's palace to be specially trained for his service (notice that even this war-mongering ruler knew the value of a great education). Interestingly, the first act of wisdom involved their dietary choices. They refused to eat the king's meat—which had not been killed according to Mosaic Law and was probably offered to a pagan god —or drink their new ruler's wine. What they chose instead was the following: *"Please test your servants for ten days: Give us nothing but vegetables to eat and water to drink"* (Daniel 1:12).

These young men, away from their parents and living in luxury at the king's palace, refused to lower the standards by which they had been raised. They did so politely, and they even offered a comparison test so their guardians would be reassured that they'd be just fine following the ways they'd been taught. And what was the result of Daniel, Shadrach, Meshach, and Abednego's training?

> *Will you look back over the years and be filled with regret and shame, or will you be ready to celebrate your membership in the "Parenting Hall of Fame?"*

"At the end of the ten days they looked healthier and better nourished than any of the young men who ate the royal food. So the guard took away their choice food and the wine they were to drink and gave them vegetables instead. To these four young men God gave knowledge and understanding of all kinds of literature and learning. And Daniel could understand visions and dreams of all kinds. At the end of the time set by the king to bring them into his service, the chief official presented them to Nebuchadnezzar...In every matter of wisdom and understanding about which the king questioned them, he found them ten times better than all the magicians and enchanters in his whole kingdom" (Daniel 1:15–18, 20).

> *Your kids will tell stories about you for years on end. What do you want those tales to include?*

The most amazing acts of faith followed these first simple steps in the legacy their parents had passed on to them.

Shadrach, Meshach, and Abednego refused to bow down before an idol and, in turn, were thrown into a fiery furnace. Yet their proclamation to the king about the God they believed in before entering the flames revealed the depth of their faith—a faith developed years before by parents whose names we don't even know (see Daniel 3 for the full story).

> *Spend some time now envisioning exactly what you'd like your family to look like in the future.*

Later we find Daniel had to make a similar stand for his beliefs. The other administrators in the palace tried to find some sort of flaw in Daniel in order to get rid of this godly man, but *"they could find no corruption in him, because he was trustworthy and neither corrupt nor negligent"* (Daniel 6:4b). This man, who'd been taken from his family and raised in a foreign land, was a person of tremendous character. Where had he learned these virtues? Who had taught him to take responsibility for his actions, be self-disciplined in all he did, and strive to please God above himself? Could it have been those unknown parents who'd made a tremendous impact in their son's life years earlier?

Of course, the jealous officials kept watching and waiting, and they caught Daniel praying to God when he was only supposed to worship the king. As a result, Daniel was thrown into a lion's den, but the Lord once again chose to deliver His faithful follower who wouldn't compromise his beliefs simply to save himself (Daniel 6 tells the entire story of God's deliverance).

> *The godly principles they seem to have imparted to their children allowed these young men to behave exceptionally when it mattered most.*

Do you remember when we told you earlier that your kids will make some of the most important decisions in their lives when you aren't around? Well, the stories of Daniel, Shadrach,

Meshach, and Abednego certainly confirm that concept! Even in the midst of life-threatening situations, they were completely confident that their God would save them, one way or another. Their faith was secure because their family had educated them in Straight Lines that would stand the test of time.

> *Their faith was secure because their family had educated them in Straight Lines that would stand the test of time.*

Evidently those parents made a huge impact on their children, and the legacy that resulted was not only a powerful witness to those around them, but it also inspires millions today who hear and read the story of these young men's lives.

Is this what you want for your kids? Do you dream great dreams for them? Is your vision for your exceptional children so clear that you can't wait to wake up each morning and keep striving for it? Are you confident that following these Straight Lines will indeed help your kids, their kids, and all the generations that follow to become exceptional human beings? Finally, are you willing to commit to living and teaching these Straight Lines *all* the way through life's journey?

> *Is this what you want for your kids? Do you dream great dreams for them? Is your vision for your exceptional children so clear that you can't wait to wake up each morning and keep striving for it?*

If so, we'd like to welcome you to the path leading to the Parenting Hall of Fame. You're on your way!

My Straight Line NAV System

Birth–5: Little ones learn best about legacy by watching you in action. They absorb everything at this stage of life, especially your tone of voice, your facial expressions, and body language. Remember, actions speak much louder than words, especially when it comes to the loving, caring environment you want them to replicate someday for their own children.

6–12: Now is the time to introduce the concept of legacy. Good choices make for a good name, and at this stage of development, your kids can learn that *everything* they do and say will impact their future! They need to understand they are making their own legacy each and every day.

13–20+: Be sure to begin the "passing the baton" process during these critical developmental years. As you continue to equip your teenagers and young adults with skill sets they need to become exceptional, talk to them about how they can pass these same godly principles on to their own children one day.

Chapter 10

Summing Up Straight Line Strategies

Several years ago, we took our sons to Europe on vacation. We earnestly believe these family times are essential for rest and relaxation, but we also feel that they are opportunities to develop the Three Pillars of Faith, Family, and Education. While we were visiting Italy, we learned about the ingenious civil engineers of ancient Rome who, over the course of several centuries, built a system of roads over 400,000 kilometers (roughly 240,000 miles), connecting Western Europe to the Middle East and beyond.

What is particularly amazing about their unprecedented roadways is that these engineers always started with a deep foundation, and they laid their streets out almost ruler-straight. Why would they take time to dig two feet into the ground for miles and miles before laying down stone, sand, and cement? Because the ancient Romans knew that for something to last, it needed a solid foundation. These architects of Roman civilization also believed that the straight-line integrity would provide optimal pathways for everyone to follow.

> *The ancient Romans knew that for something to last, it needed a solid foundation.*

It shouldn't be too surprising to us in modern society that some of these Roman roads, which linked its one hundred and thirteen provinces, are still used millennia later. Called via, or "the way," each road was painstakingly designed, beginning with initial planning, surveying, then building and developing. Many sections took years to complete, but the end result was an exceptional thoroughfare which would stand the test of time.

For your authors, this experience was another *wow!* moment in the parenting process. As we stood on one of these Roman roadways, we wondered if the foundation we had been laying down for our two boys would be solid years later. We thought about the Straight Lines we so firmly believed in and contemplated whether or not they'd still be followed by the generations that are going to follow us one day. If we were as diligent about all our labors as these ancient developers had been, would our legacy stand the test of time, too?

> *Your children will have the opportunity to grow and develop in amazing ways as you intentionally implement these concepts in your lives and homes.*

After years of effort and energy, with our two sons and with thousands of other families, we are more convinced than ever that the nine Straight Line Strategies we've shared with you will indeed pave the road to success for your family. Your children will have the opportunity to grow and develop in amazing ways as you intentionally implement these concepts in your lives and homes.

So, let's spend a little time reflecting on these Straight Lines and some final goals for raising exceptional children.

Walk This Way

At the beginning of this book, we quoted an interesting proverb from the Old Testament. It reads:

Summing Up Straight Line Strategies

"Listen, my son, accept what I say, and the years of your life will be many. I instruct you in the way of wisdom and lead you along straight paths. When you walk, your steps will not be hampered; when you run, you will not stumble" (Proverbs 4:10–12).

In Proverbs, King Solomon shared some of the strategies for success he'd discovered during life's journey. Notice that he used the analogy of "straight paths" as he talked about winning in all vital areas of life. And what is the reward for traveling down these time-tested roadways? Unhampered steps, unlikely stumbling, and years of satisfaction and success!

> *Exceptional parents intentionally strive for an exceptional future for their kids.*

What parents wouldn't want these blessings bestowed upon each of their children? Exceptional parents intentionally strive for an exceptional future for their kids—a future full of opportunity and potentially free of many unnecessary problems and pain.

But parents, as we've stated before, this exceptional parenting process won't happen without your active participation. As we have demonstrated, it demands your time, energy, and unswerving effort. Tremendous planning, prayer, and hands-on parenting from birth into adulthood will be integral to the optimal success of your children.

Notice that King Solomon, known as the wisest man to have ever lived, carefully spelled out his advice for the next generation. He added to this strategy for success with these thoughts:

> *Think about where you are going, don't get side-tracked from good guidelines for living, stay away from bad things, and keep focused on forward progress.*

"Let your eyes look straight ahead; fix your gaze directly before you. Give careful thought to the paths for your feet and be steadfast in all your ways.

Do not turn to the right or the left; keep your foot from evil" (*Proverbs 4:25–27*).

If you look at the concepts Solomon detailed, they seem quite simple: think about where you are going, don't get sidetracked from good guidelines for living, stay away from bad things, and keep focused on forward progress. Wow! Isn't this exactly what we desire for our babies, toddlers, children, teenagers, and young adults? These principles don't seem too complex, but the benefits for training and equipping our kids with them will be unbelievable! Like this wise ruler, we simply need to intentionally train them to "walk this way," and then show them by our regular, consistent example exactly how to do just that.

> *What should a "fully developed adult" look like? What behaviors would he or she exhibit? How would others view him or her?*

FOUR FINAL GOALS FOR YOUR EXCEPTIONAL KIDS

When parents get the first glimpse of their newborn baby, they imagine all sorts of possibilities that await this boy or girl in the future. No one we've ever known has said to us, "Oh, I sure hope my child turns out to be average." Quite the opposite! At this stage of life, parents are thinking big and dreaming even bigger. Their vision for the future is boundless, and they're excited about discovering all that is exceptional about their precious child.

But somewhere along life's journey, many parents lose this initial burst of energy and enthusiasm. They tend to stray from the original Straight Lines they envisioned to get their child to become a motivated, curious, caring, competent individual who will one day not only exceed expectations but also become an inspiring member of his or her community.

So, it's essential for all parents to focus on four final goals that are critical for launching their children into the world. Our exceptional children must be:

1. Mature
2. Wise
3. Leaders
4. Servants

> *As children build Relational Equity with God and their family, they'll tend to want to make choices that won't hurt those who care about them most.*

Throughout this book we have discussed Straight Line Strategies that will guide you in the parenting process, yet these final goals must be part of the "end game" that you're seeking as exceptional parents. Let's take a closer look at each one of them.

MATURE

Maturity is an interesting and sometimes elusive word in today's society. It involves showing mental, emotional, and physical characteristics that are associated with a fully developed person. Think about that for a moment. What should a "fully developed adult" look like? What behaviors would he or she exhibit? How would others view him or her?

With fruit on a tree or vegetables in a garden, a husbandman carefully tends and monitors the produce until it's perfectly ripe and ready to be of use in the world. In a similar way, parents must prepare their children to function as mature adults one day in the future.

WISE

Wisdom is another essential skill that parents should be developing over time. Some children will have more of a natural ability than others to make sensible decisions and choices, but even the most gifted in good judgment will need guidance along life's journey to enhance these skill sets. For those kids who struggle in this area, parents need to be extremely vigilant and help them understand what good judgment looks like.

The Three Pillars of Parenting are fundamental elements that will assist our children in the process of becoming wise. When they understand God's guidelines for great living, kids begin to make those their own. As children build Relational Equity with God and their family, they'll tend to want to make choices that won't hurt those who care about them most. Finally, the education of boys and girls not only builds upon their strengths and improves any weaknesses, but it also develops their overall wisdom.

LEADERS

In our business, LEADon, we've been privileged to work with thousands of leaders. Through these experiences, we've discovered a similar theme: leaders aren't just born, they are made over time. As with wisdom, some people have a more innate ability for leadership than others, but the skill sets for becoming a good leader can and should be developed within every one of our children.

> *Leaders aren't just born, they are made over time. Some people have a more innate ability for leadership than others, but the skill sets for becoming a good leader can and should be developed within every one of our children.*

Leadership involves being willing and able to take a stand for what is right, no matter what anyone else around you thinks or feels. Leadership also includes the ability to guide, direct, and influence people. This is extremely important when you consider the legacy you hope to leave behind, not only in your children, but also in future generations.

As leaders, your children must be able to pass on the principles of Faith,

Family, and Education to their own kids one day. They must be able to "guide, direct, and influence" the next generation so these Straight Lines will continue to be followed for years to come.

(While we wish we had more time to delve into leadership skill sets here; for now we will refer you to our book, *The Leading Edge: 9 Strategies for Improving Internal and Intentional Leadership*).

SERVANTS

Finally, exceptional parents will instill in their children a desire to become servants in the world around them. While there has certainly been a complex history with the term "serve," in essence, it means to give of oneself to another. Members of the armed forces serve their country. Customer service is extremely valued in outstanding businesses. People who provide acts of service for their community are highly esteemed.

> *Leadership also includes the ability to guide, direct, and influence people.*

Parents should be developing this type of attitude, or "heart to serve," in their children. Moms and dads need to give their kids as many opportunities as they can to practice service in their own homes, schools, churches, and communities. Once again, continuing to focus on the Three Pillars of Parenting you've been reading about will assist you in building up this important area for your future adults.

> *While there has certainly been a complex history with the term "serve," in essence, it means to give of oneself to another.*

We are now reaping many rewarding *wow!* moments as parents of young adults, and these are a direct result of the nine Straight Lines that have guided us since their infancy. We recently received copies of letters of recommendation each one received from their respective mentors. We could barely keep back the tears as we read about their good judgment and character, and we were so pleased to discover that these mentors had observed maturity, wisdom, and servant-leadership in each of our sons. You, too, can enjoy similar results!

Keeping these four final goals in mind, can you picture each of your children one day as mature, wise leaders who serve in such a way that they are an inspiration in their families and communities? If not, catch a glimpse of that vision today. Write these four goals in a place where you will view them often, and set goals for your parenting that will enhance each of these in the days, weeks, and months ahead. If you do, you will have many of your own *wow!* moments in the future.

> *Parents should be developing this type of attitude, or "heart to serve," in their children. Moms and dads need to give their kids as many opportunities as they can to practice service in their own homes, schools, churches, and communities.*

THE STRAIGHT LINE COVENANT FOR YOUR FAMILY

Over the past several decades, we've learned so much while raising our children, and these lessons have sharpened our skills as parents and as professionals. We've been able to carry many of these strategies into the corporate world where we discovered that they're just as sound and effective as they are in our own lives and homes. Why? Because Straight Lines are transcendent truths!

One strategy we've used with numerous "corporate families" is that of a covenant. A covenant is a solemn agreement that all parties promise to abide by. For an organization, we ask leaders and employees to agree to follow

> *Over the past several decades, we've learned so much while raising our children.*

Summing Up Straight Line Strategies

a set of principles for the ultimate benefit of the organization (in the *Resources* section you'll see our book, *Corporate Family Matters: Creating and Developing Organizational Dynasties*).

In the case of your personal family, a covenant agreement would greatly enhance the implementation

> *Parents, these are the guidelines to get your kids from average to great.*

of the Straight Line Strategies you've been learning about and implementing in your lives. At the end of this chapter, we will provide you with our version of a Family Covenant, but in the meantime, let's take a few minutes to review the nine Straight Lines we've been sharing:

Strategy #1: *Raising motivated, inspirational kids that exceed expectations is a direct result of moms and dads who are intentional about following specific "Straight Lines" throughout the parenting process.*

Strategy #2: *Faith is pivotal to developing exceptional kids. Parents need to build their lives on the Lord's principles so that these can be taught to and "caught" by their children.*

Strategy #3: *Developing your family unit begins with Relational Equity. This is the one equity that children will not stray from as they journey through life.*

Strategy #4: *Discipline is about passing on good decision-making to the next generation. These skill sets must begin at home, and then they can be honed in real world experiences over time.*

> *The nine Straight Line Strategies will do more than simply help them make it through life—they'll allow them to thrive!*

Strategy #5: *Learning to relate with God, family, friends, and other people is an essential skill that will help every child experience life in exceptional ways. That's because Relationship is the Center of our Universe!*

Strategy #6: *Parents' primary focus must be on becoming an expert in their kids. Only then can the educational process make its most powerful impact.*

Strategy #7: *Exceptional parents make personal responsibility a value. Demonstrating good judgment and making wise choices are among the most important virtues you can teach your children.*

Strategy #8: *Parents must actively provide opportunities for their children to learn through daily, real-life experiences.*

Strategy #9: *Exceptional parents intentionally encourage their children to pass the Straight Lines for being exceptional to the next generation.*

> *By emphasizing the Pillars of Faith, Family, and Education found within these strategies, your children will have a solid foundation to build their future upon and pass on to the generations of family members who will follow.*

Parents, these are the guidelines to get your kids from average to great. These are the pathways that will help you develop your children into exceptional adults. The nine Straight Line Strategies will do more than simply help them make it through life—they'll allow them to thrive!

Of all the things you've been trying to do to help your kids be successful, you can now hone in on these Straight Lines. By emphasizing the Pillars of Faith, Family, and Education found within these strategies, your children

Summing Up Straight Line Strategies

will have a solid foundation to build their future upon and pass on to the generations of family members who will follow.

It's up to you as exceptional parents to seek the Lord for His guidance on how to best raise your children. After all, we believe He created each of your kids as unique and amazing human beings who will live for eternity. God has gifted you with their presence, and He has also given you the ultimate responsibility for their upbringing. It's a huge responsibility, and one each of us must take seriously.

> *It's up to you as exceptional parents to seek the Lord for His guidance on how to best raise your children.*

The wonderful news is that God has promised to be with us throughout the entire parenting process. He also offers us godly principles in the Bible to help us along the way. One of our favorite verses on parenting is from the book of Proverbs:

"*Trust in the LORD with all your heart and lean not on your own understanding; in all your ways submit to him, and he will make your paths straight*" (3:5–6).

Our God, the Creator and expert of Straight Lines, asks us to do the very best we can, and then we are simply to trust! He alone has the power to straighten our paths as we submit to His directions for safe, secure, and successful living here on Earth. While we may not clearly understand His purpose for various circumstances, we can rest in the fact that He has a perfect plan in mind.

> *When things get tough, get tougher! Ask the Lord for help, then do what needs to be done for the benefit of your children.*

So, keep working hard! Continue learning and growing as an individual and parent. Deepen your faith. Strengthen your family. Educate yourselves and your children. When things get tough, get tougher! Ask the

Lord for help, then do what needs to be done for the benefit of your children. Finally, trust—trust in the great God who loves you and your kids, for He indeed has an amazing future planned for all of you!

Summing Up Straight Line Strategies

Our Family's Straight Line Covenant

1. All family members will strive to be motivated, inspirational people who exceed expectations. We will intentionally follow Straight Lines.

2. We will develop our Faith by following the Lord's principles for godly living.

3. Relational Equity will be an integral virtue in our family unit.

4. All family members will strive to be Self-Disciplined, making good choices that proudly represent our Family and Faith.

5. Because Relationships are the Center of the Universe, we will interact with others in our world in healthy, positive ways.

6. Education will be valued by all family members, and we will work on enhancing strengths and improving weaknesses.

7. Everyone in our family will take Personal Responsibility for our words and actions.

8. Since real-life experiences are essential for growth and development, we will regularly and consistently get involved in our community to learn more about our world.

9. Our family name and legacy are critical to long-term success, so we will strive each day to be exceptional human beings who will positively impact our world and future generations.

Resources

Ames, L.B., Ilg, F.L., & Baker, S.M. (1988). *Your Ten-to Fourteen-Year-Old.* New York: Dell Trade Paperback. (*Dr. Ames and her colleagues have many books for different age groups).

Armstrong, T. (1999). *7 Kinds of Smart: Indentifying and Developing Your Multiple Intelligences.* New York: Plume.

Bledsoe, M. (2002). *Parenting with Dignity.* New York: Alpha Books.

Brazelton, T.B., & Greenspan, S.I. (2000). *The Incredible Needs of Children: What Every Child Must Have to Grow, Learn, And Flourish.* New York: Perseus Publishing.

Carder, D. (1991). *Secrets of Your Family Tree: Healing the Present In Light of the Past.* Chicago, IL: Moody Press.

Cloud, H., & Townsend, J. (2001). *Boundaries with Kids: How Healthy Choices Grow Healthy Children.* Grand Rapids, MI: Zondervan.

DePorter, B. (2006). *Quantum Success: 8 Key Catalysts to Shift Your Energy into Dynamic Focus.* Oceanside, CA: Learning Forum Publications.

Dobson, J. (1996). *The New Dare to Discipline.* Carol Stream, IL: Tyndale House Publishers.

Dobson, J. (1999). *The New Hide or Seek: Building Self-Esteem in Your Child* (3rded.).Grand Rapids: Fleming H. Revell Company.

Dobson, J. (2001). *Bringing Up Boys: Practical Advice and Encouragement for Those Shaping the Next Generation of Men.* Carol Stream, IL: Tyndale House Publishers.

Dobson, J. (2007). *Parenting Isn't for Cowards: The 'You Can Do It' Guide for Hassled Parents from America's Best-Loved Family Advocate.* Carol Stream, IL: Tyndale House Publishers.

Dobson, J. (2010). *Bringing Up Girls: Practical Advice and Encouragement for Those Shaping the Next Generation of Women.* Carol Stream, IL: Tyndale House Publishers.

Durman, T. (2009). *Bite-Sized Wisdom for Parents with Kids Ages Two Through Twenty.* Koloa, Hawaii: Two to Twenty Publishing.

Elkind, D. (2006). *The Hurried Child—25th Anniversary Edition.* Cambridge, MA: Da Capo Press.

Gardner, H. (2011). *Frames of Mind: the Theory of Multiple Intelligences.* New York: Basic Books.

Goleman, D. (2006). *Emotional Intelligence: 10th Anniversary Edition; Why It Can Matter More Than IQ.* New York: Bantam.

Kimmel, T. (2004). *Grace-Based Parenting.* Nashville, TN: Thomas Nelson.

Kimmel, T. (2006). *Raising Kids for True Greatness: Redefine Success for You and Your Child.* Nashville, TN: Thomas Nelson.

McDowell, J. (2008). *The Father Connection: How You Can Make the Difference in Your Child's Self-Esteem and Sense of Purpose.* Nashville, TN: B&H Publishing Group.

Thomas, G. (2005). *Sacred Parenting: How Raising Children Shapes Our Souls.* Grand Rapids, MI: Zondervan.

Wilke, S., & Wilke, R. (2010). *Corporate Family Matters: Creating and Developing Organizational Dynasties.* San Diego: LEADon, Inc.

Wilke, S., & Wilke, R. (2010). *The Leading Edge: 9 Strategies for Improving Internal and Intentional Leadership.* San Diego: LEADon, Inc.

Wright, H.N. (1991). *The Power of a Parent's Words.* Ventura, CA: Regal Books.

About the Authors

Steve Wilke is founder and director of the Family Counseling Center which has served the Southern California area for three decades. Rebecca Wilke is an Educational and Leadership Coach and has worked in public, private, and university settings. Drs. Wilke also own and operate Sonkist Ministries and LEADon, Inc., a leadership development company.

Through LEADon, Drs. Wilke equip twenty-first century leaders with time-tested skill sets, including:

* Personal and Professional Life Balance
* Transformational Leadership
* Conflict Resolution
* Building High-Performance Teams
* Developing Corporate Culture

In addition to authoring numerous books, Drs. Wilke speak nationally and internationally, and they enjoy sharing their leadership skill sets via the Internet, radio, and television.

Sonkist Publishing, P.O. Box 503377 San Diego, CA 92150
www.sonkist.com